WHAT

RADICAL

HUSBANDS

DO

12 STEPS TO WIN AND KEEP
YOUR WIFE'S HEART

REGI CAMPBELL

PRSS

What Radical Husbands Do
12 Steps to Win and Keep Your Wife's Heart
Published by RM Press
1155 Mt. Vernon Hwy
Suite 800
Atlanta, GA 30338

The graphic above is a registered trademark of RM Press.

The website addresses recommended in this book are offered as a resource to you.

ISBN 978-0-9916074-0-2
eISBN 978-0-9916074-1-9

Published in association with the nonprofit Radical Mentoring, 1155 Mt. Vernon Hwy, Suite 800, Atlanta, GA 30338

The Team: Regi Campbell, Daniel Kosmala
Cover Design: Russell Shaw

Printed in the United States of America
First Edition 2014

"When I think of my best days as husband, I find I was doing what Regi said in this book. *What Radical Husbands Do* is a practical book I can safely give any man who is struggling in his marriage."

— **JOEL MANBY,** CEO of Herschend Family Entertainment, author of *Love Works*, and star of an "Undercover Boss" episode on CBS

"Guys, let's face it. We're good at winning a lot of things, but a woman's heart? Where do we begin? Seriously, what does that even mean? That's where my friend Regi Campbell's wonderful new book, *What Radical Husbands Do*, comes in. This ain't theory. This is a proven strategy (yes, strategy) for reengaging with your wife at a level you may not have known was even possible. Regi's been teaching this material to our men for years. I'm so grateful he's chosen to make it available to a broader audience."

— **ANDY STANLEY,** Author, Speaker and Presenter, "Your Move" on NBC

"All husbands need men, who are a "little down the road," to speak into their lives and marriage. That's what reading Regi's Campbell's book, *What Radical Husband's Do*, is all about. It is like sitting across the table from a wise "man's man" who wants the best for your marriage. Through refreshing transparency, real stories, practical applications, hard truths, and amazing grace, Regi shows the real life way to your wife's heart."

— **TED LOWE,** Founder of MarriedPeople, co-author of *MarriedPeople, How Your Church Can Build Marriages That Last*

"Regi is a thorough and thoughtful companion in the inevitable tough places of marriage. His candid approach is brave and calls on the resilience of his readers. I look forward to recommending this for husbands who want a better marriage and are wanting wise, practical guidance."

— **KATHY MALCOLM HALL,** Licensed Professional Counselor

"*What Radical Husbands Do* is the most practical book for rebuilding a marriage that I have ever read. It's perfect for any man wanting to save his marriage."

— **BILL JONES,** President, Columbia International University

"Regi is used of God to speak behind the masks men wear. He understands the lies we tell ourselves and shows us how we can allow others into that place to begin to alter the permission we give ourselves to fail. He teaches men, how to gain trusted permission, and how to speak with truth, grace and compassion. He directs men into true, life-giving freedom! I could not more highly endorse a book or friend more."

— **JOHN LYNCH,** Author of *On My Worst Day* and co-author of *The Cure* and *Bo's Cafe*

"Direct, straightforward manual for identifying problems and concrete, doable steps for customizing solutions that will work. Non-sugar coated, "tell it like it is" book that will reshape and benefit many lives."

— **BRENDA JONES,** Happily married to Ted for 36 years

"I first 'met' Regi through About My Father's Business - a book that launched my faith at work. I later had the great opportunity to be mentored by him in one of his Radical Mentoring groups - where Regi impacted me, my wife and my children in a really meaningful way. Now Regi has distilled some of the most powerful and time-tested marriage lessons for today's man in *What Radical Husbands Do.* I highly recommend this book to any guy looking for some practical advice on how he can 'own' the success of his marriage."

— **DAVE KATZ,** SVP, Coca-Cola Consolidated

"A raw, witty life lesson on how to win a wife's heart … spoken by a true leader who missed it, then lived it … no fluff, no quick tricks, but a fundamental choice to be different, a choice to excel at home, like he did at work … spoken by a real man, for men. Are you ready? "

— **PEYTON DAY,** CEO, ROAM Innovative Workplaces

"Finally a straightforward book for men who are serious about their marriage and not only want to be a better spouse, but a better man. Campbell provides a no excuses approach with logical and practical next steps. This book is a great tool for marriage counselors and husbands wanting to improve their marriage."

— **RACHEL HOLCOMB,** Licensed Counselor,
Director of Mentoring Systems, NPCC

"When it comes to something as important as marriage it is vital to get it right! I found the message to be hard hitting, straightforward, honest and compelling. Not your average marriage advice book, this book is born of personal experience and built on practical advice. The application was clear and is drawn from the actual experience of the author. If you care about your marriage and family, you owe it to them and yourself to learn from someone who knows what he is talking about. And it might just RADICALLY transform your marriage… life… and future!"

— **DAVID SALYERS,** SVP, Chick-Fil-A and
Co-author, *Remarkable!*

"Regi's passion for this subject and his experiences, both personal and those garnered through mentoring others, comes through in such a useful way. Impactful book; much of which I had to endure while wincing…"Thank you Sir, may I have another."

— **ROCKY BUTLER,** CEO, Alliance Precision Plastics

"I like Regi's writing style . . . honest, humble, real, practical, hopeful but it also does not sugar-coat just how hard this can be. I think this book will be an excellent resource for men with good marriages, bad marriages and everything in-between. I also like the fact that it is action oriented. When a man's marriage is dying, he needs practical steps that he can immediately take, not a change of his character which could takes months or years to happen. The practical steps will hopefully provide the means for the change of character to happen and it can save (or at least improve) his marriage in the meantime."

— **BOBBY REAGAN,** Principal, Reagan Consulting

TABLE OF CONTENTS

PREFACE

his is a book written to men. I'm a man, and what I have to say is to men.

It's a book about marriage. Your marriage. Not her marriage. Not their marriage. *Your* marriage.

What I have to say starts with a premise. Not everyone will buy into my premise but I'm okay with that. Here it is . . .

The man determines the quality of his marriage.

It's not up to your wife. It's not up to the two of you together. It's up to you.

Why? Because *you only control you.* You're the only variable in the equation you get to fill in. And you can't change the other variables. You can't change your wife, your mother-in-law or the past. You only control you . . . what you think, what you say and what you do.

Winning your wife's heart is everything. It is to marriage what the secret formula is to Coke. Win her heart and keep it and everything else is easy, or at least easier. You can substitute the word "desires" if you'd like. When you've won her heart, her "desires" are for you and your marriage.

It's up to you to win and keep your wife's heart. You can't trade for it. There's not a fixed amount of effort required. There's no way to "get there" and then quit. There's not even a guarantee you'll succeed, no matter what you do.

Every marriage has bliss. Days and seasons when it *just works*. You both get what you want, you talk about things, sex is frequent and fabulous, and you're as happy as a man can be.

Yet every marriage gets lost somewhere along the way. Some get found, some don't. It happens to everyone. You're frustrated, bored, seduced, angry, lazy or exhausted. You want out. You'd rather be alone than in this mess. When asked if she ever contemplated divorce, Ruth Graham (Billy Graham's wife) said, "No, I've never thought of divorce in all these 35 years of marriage; but I did think of murder a few times."[1] At some point in your marriage, it'll seem like anything would be better than this. If it hasn't happened yet, it will.

If you're lost, the first thing you have to do is figure out where you are. Being dead-level honest, ***where is your marriage right now?*** If it's working, it takes a nano-second to answer. Your question is, *How do I keep it going?* If it's bad, you also don't have to think very long. You're so frustrated, you may have no idea what to do next. For everyone else, it may not be quite so clear. You may be somewhere in the middle. . . . it's not as great as it once was, but not as bad as most of your friends' marriages.

This book will offer up 12 steps you can take to save your marriage if it's in trouble, to make it great if it's good, and to make it better if it's just okay.

Now, I don't have all the answers. I don't know your wife. Your past. Your specific situation. Your willingness or ability to adapt. Your level of arrogance versus your level of humility. I'm not a psychologist, counselor or a trained marriage expert, but I do know what worked for me. And over the past 13 years, I've watched it work over and over again as I've shared it with a bunch of other guys.

A WORD TO THE WIVES
I've been around long enough to know that women get real curious about books their men read, probably because we read less than you do. I have three

things to say to the "maverick" wife who might be reading this, especially if you're a wife who is hanging by a thread on the other end of a failing marriage.

First, don't give up and get out. If he's been unfaithful, get out of the house or get him out. You both need space. You both need time to process what's happened, and you'll be hard pressed to think clearly in the same house with the same routine. My wife leaving was the best thing to ever happen to me. It was the wake-up call I needed. Her motive was pure. She didn't leave to pay me back or get even or teach me a lesson. She left so she could think. Pray. Gain perspective. She didn't leave as a first step toward separation and divorce. She left as a first step toward clarity for herself. But it gave me time to find clarity also. And that clarity led to my recycling. More on that later.

Secondly, know there are no such things as "marriage problems." We have personal problems, revealed in the white-hot heat of marriage. He has some and you have some. If he's coming to realize some of his "issues" . . . starting to accept them and take ownership . . . and there's sincere humility and conviction in his heart, you're an idiot to abandon this marriage. He's on his way to becoming the man you wanted and thought you married to begin with. Give him some time and encouragement. What's rewarded is repeated. You get what you glorify. So catch him when he does stuff right and brag on him. Baby steps can lead to giant leaps, given the right encouragement.

And you may need to get some outside perspective on your issues. Yes, you have issues, and some of them have helped make your marriage what it is. Do what you want him to do . . . get someone to help you see yourself, to help you open yourself up and look at what needs attention. The best way to heal your marriage is to find healing for yourself. And as I'll say repeatedly to the men, whatever you do to improve yourself will pay dividends, no matter what happens in your marriage.

Finally, if your marriage is in trouble, know your challenge will be forgiving and forgetting. You may be totally justified in throwing the bum out or taking off. What he's done, what he's said, his selfishness, his constant criticism . . . maybe all of the above . . . any rational woman would get out and start over. But now he's ready to try . . . really try to make things different. He's using different words. There's an earnestness that hasn't been there. If you see this kind of movement on his part, you're smart to move toward him and see what comes of it. After all, do you really want to start over and train another hard-headed man to be a decent husband? It's so much better for you, the kids, your folks, for everyone, if this marriage becomes rock solid.

SO GET READY MEN . . .

This is going to be straight-up, in-your-face and honest. Can you take the truth? Will you recognize the things that kill a marriage and make a real effort to go in a better direction?

Will you do what it takes to become a RADICAL HUSBAND?

HOW'S YOUR MARRIAGE
REALLY?

"Your present circumstances don't determine where you can
go; they merely determine where you start."
– Nido Qubein

I'm a guy who's been hanging on to his marriage for almost 45 years — by a thread. If there were ever two people not prepared for marriage, it was us. Two twenty-year-old college sophomores, infatuated and hot for each other. Raised in homes where you only had sex after you were married and divorce was out of the question, we announced we were getting married in August. We had met the previous September and started dating in February. We tied the knot after dating for only six months. We hardly knew each other, and worse, the dense fog of intense infatuation veiled our deep differences.

We differed on everything — *everything*. She was a pessimist; I was an optimist. She was fearful; I was fearless. I was extroverted; she was introverted. I wanted to party; she just wanted to be with me. I was A.D.D.; she did one thing at a time. She cared immensely what people thought; I didn't give a rip! She enjoyed beauty and wanted to "smell the roses"; I was in a hurry and didn't even notice the dang flowers. She was a perfectionist; I did just enough to get by. She loved houses and decorating; I couldn't have cared less. I could go on for pages about our differences. Those who know us, even today, say they've never seen two people more different.

Once we were married, the sexual pressure was released and things rolled along well for a while. Sex had been a dirty word in her house and her reluctance soon became apparent. My sex education had been, "Keep it in your pants, boy — until you're married!" Now that we were married and it was legal, I wanted sex all the time. And she yielded; for a long time she yielded. But there was less and less intimacy. More routine . . . and resentment.

Eighteen months after our wedding, she faced student teaching at the university. Her supervisor was so intimidating, Miriam literally fainted one day under the pressure. She went into survival mode, doing everything she could to please this supervisor and get through the semester. She had nothing left for me, but instead of rallying behind her, I turned on her. I interpreted the lack of attention (i.e., lack of sex) as rejection and I was angry. A pattern was set that carried on for the next 12 years.

Anger comes from unmet demands and the more she didn't meet my demands, the angrier I got. What's worse, I didn't release the anger; I harbored it. I kept it in the dark where it could grow. I quietly seethed. I loved her, especially when she did what I wanted. But when she didn't, I was manipulative, critical, sarcastic and downright mean. By this time, we were college seniors and had been social drinkers for a couple of years. I took it to another level, thinking I was numbing my anger, but actually making it worse.

The years went by. We morphed from college to career, marrieds to parents, and renters to homeowners. We made all the transitions couples make. From the outside, we looked like the happy little couple with two happy little kids. We went to church, took trips, worked in the yard. We looked like everyone else. But our relationship was steadily worsening. I wanted sex. She wanted intimacy. I didn't have time for intimacy; I was going to school at night, working on my MBA, climbing the corporate ladder. I worked hard and wanted to play hard. She cared for two little kids all day, every day and wanted rest. (We had at least one in diapers for five straight years). She wanted the perfect house, with just the right tile in the bathroom. The tiles all looked the same to me.

Eventually, it all crashed.

I had married the wrong woman. The differences were just too great and she wouldn't even try to change. She saw me as a corporate "hoe," willing to sacrifice her, the kids . . . *anything* . . . to get ahead. She had submissively moved five times in nine years and the last one took a huge toll. I'd accepted a job far away from her hometown, her mother and her sisters, and I had done it without even talking to her. I simply announced it.

In a particularly lucid conversation one night, she looked at me and said, "Regi, we have different dreams." She was leaving me. "Get to know your kids," she said, and walked out the door.

Not once had I thought she might leave.

Stupid me.

That night, and over the next few days, I got clarity for the first time.

I had taken her *completely* for granted. I had assigned no value to what she meant to me. What she did for me, for our kids or for our home.

The old saying, "absence makes the heart grow fonder," is true.

Over the next week, I realized what I had. I looked myself in the mirror and didn't like what I saw. I saw an angry 33-year-old, drinking to hide his anger, married to a beautiful woman who simply wanted a home and a family. I decided that if I could get a do-over, a second chance, I could be happy. And I could make her happy.

But there was a problem.

Twelve years of career worship, corporate moves, selfishness and insensitivity had driven Miriam away. I had created an environment of criticism and rejection — a place where she never measured up. I had subtly threatened to abandon her. I had been restless and unhappy. Now I thought I could be content. Now I wanted to commit to her. But she was gone.

Before she left, I had been a good dad. But now, having the kids all by myself, I fell in love with them all over again, and in a deeper way. I saw I could be a great dad and we could have a great family, if only she'd give me another shot.

In the loneliness of her leaving, I started thinking about all the good instead of the bad. I thought of all the things *she did* and started to forget about the things I'd "tried and convicted" her of *not doing*. I knew I could stop criticizing her. I was ready to accept her as she was and ready to stop trying to change her.

That was the birthplace of this book. Miriam did come back, agreeing to stay one day. She said, "You're saying different things, but your voice sounds the same." Interpretation? "You're saying words I haven't heard before, and there's a sincerity that's unfamiliar. But the sound of your voice tells me it's still **you.**" She decided to come back and check it out. After that day, I asked if she'd stay another day. She agreed. Then another.

It's been 31 years now. I'm still on a day-to-day contract.

I had to take *radical* action. I had one day to win her heart. That "win" got me another day. Ever so slowly, she warmed up to me, and it got better and better from there.

You see, it was my chance to *win* her love for the first time. When we first met, it was easy. It was chemistry . . . infatuation . . . hormones. This time, it was going to take effort — second effort, third effort, endless effort. Even though the "day-to-day contract" has become a light-hearted euphemism, it reminds me that my marriage is up to me. It will become what I make it. I am responsible. I am the leader. Love isn't a hole I fall into; it's a choice I make.

YOUR STORY ISN'T MY STORY

That's what happened to me. Not for a minute do I think your marriage is like mine. No way. But it's not what I think that matters. The question is: "How do you feel about your marriage?" I want you to find the same clarity about your marriage as you find about your weight. Get up in the morning, step on the scales, stand still for a minute and you're going to know your weight. You can lie to yourself about whether you ate one or "just a few" Oreos. About whether your last workout was a week ago or a month ago. But put your bare feet on the scales and the truth comes out. I wish there was a machine like that for marriages, one that would tell us where things really stand.

But since it hasn't been invented yet, we'll use a different approach. I'm now going to give you snapshots of different marriages and ask if you see yourself in any of them. You'll need to be patient because a lot of these aren't you . . . but stick with me. You might find something that hits close to home.

1. **You wake up feeling lucky (or blessed, depending on your point of view) because your marriage is so good.** You get along great. You talk things out. You believe the best about each other. You're giving and getting focused attention. It feels good. Sex is frequent and there's no pressure. There's little criticism. When friends ask how it's going at home, you answer, *Couldn't be better!* . . . and you mean it.

It's rare and it's never permanent, but there are times when it's just about perfect. As good as it gets. A husband and wife working together on their marriage and on themselves as individuals. It's a season . . . a really good one, but still a season.

Here's what's going on when you're in that "good place":

- There's open communication, even about tough stuff like sex.

- Conflicts are resolved without a lot of emotion.

- You work together smoothly making plans, solving problems and making decisions.

- You have a shared vision for your marriage and family. You both know what you want it to look like, and you're willing to make individual sacrifices to make it happen.

- You've figured out your roles, with the "blessing" of the other. There's little conflict about who (normally) does what and a clear willingness to have each other's backs in emergencies.

- There's a healthy level of respect, never threatened by disagreements on small stuff. No one yells. No one pouts. You work stuff out.

- Each accepts the other *as he or she is.* No one's trying to change anyone. And each spouse tries to not take "personal" things innocently said. When feelings get hurt, you talk it through quickly, repair the relationship and move on. You don't hold grudges.

So how rare is this? There is not a marriage on earth that totally measures up to all that. There'll always be "soft spots" and things to strengthen. And people change. Sometimes we grow, sometimes regress, but we never stay the same. And while the stars can align for a while, it's nearly impossible to stay "great" all the time. Some would say it's not even healthy, but it sure sounds appealing, doesn't it?

If your marriage sounds like this, consider these 12 steps to keep it going and growing. Perhaps you'll see a few things to look out for . . . things you can do to avoid becoming overconfident, or going to sleep at the switch and sliding into "okay."

2. Your marriage is "okay." Things are stable. Consistent. There's general harmony, peace, cooperation and collaboration. There's a routine to life together. Could be you're both so busy, you don't have time to think about your marriage as a "thing." It "is what it is," so why bother? *We're making it. We're getting by. My marriage is fine. We rarely fight. We love each other. We're nowhere near the messy stuff you've described so far. There's no war going on here.*

Be grateful you're not at war.

But peace is not defined by the absence of war. Nor is a great marriage defined by the absence of conflict. It's easy to take things and people for granted. Sometimes what feels like peace to you may feel like boredom to her.

Take the case of my friend who sent a document to the printer at his house. When he reached for the tray, a document was already there. He picked it up and it just about knocked him over. It was a copy of an email his wife sent to her mentor talking about him. She says she doesn't love him anymore. She doesn't "feel it." She's tired of being taken for granted and wonders what happened to the man who wooed her like the Queen of Sheba.

Or you might have a good marriage that never becomes great because you took it easy and settled for status quo. If you think it's good just because you're getting what you want, put a hold on that. Your wife might say your marriage isn't anywhere close to where you think it is. In fact, surveys show

- Women are less happy in their marriages than men

- Women are more likely than men to see problems in their marriages

- Women are more likely to initiate divorce (women ask for divorce two-thirds of the time), and are more than three times as likely as their former husbands to have strongly desired the divorce [2]

I don't want you to turn around someday and say: *Man, I wish someone had woke me up. I was asleep at the switch. There was a storm going on. . . . I just didn't see it.*

Here are a few more things that might happen in an "okay" marriage:

- You were invited on a marriage retreat, but you blew it off because you knew it would cost money and take time away from work. Your thought was, *Nah . . . we don't need that stuff. We're doing just fine.* You knew your wife wanted to go, but you passed. Refused to seriously consider it.

- For Christmas, your dad gave you a book about how to love your wife. You thanked him politely and then put it on the shelf beside the family Bible and the Encyclopedia Britannica. Other guys have suggested books to you. You don't even write down the titles. You don't need that crap; you're doing fine.

- You're so confident in your wife's love that you're ignoring her, putting everything into your work. For a little while, that was fine. But it's become standard. And you're into your work because you're getting strokes, bonuses and promotions. She likes the money part for sure, but if you asked, she'd rather have more of you. Because you're so confident in how great things are and you're afraid you'll have to do something different, you're not going to ask.

This is the stuff guys do when they see their marriages as "okay." And I'd like to think this is where most of us are . . . right in the middle. But the divorce rate is 57%, and I keep getting blindsided by friends whose "okay" marriages are blowing up.

I want to shake you out of "okay." To wake you up. To show you how to avoid being stunned someday when "okay" is replaced with "goodbye." Let's take it the other way. Let's raise okay to *outstanding.*

3. **Your marriage is a struggle . . . or worse.** There's friction and frustration almost daily. You argue over big things and little things. The "d" word (divorce) comes up . . . a lot. Both you and she spend time thinking about what life might be like with a fresh start. You're struggling and have been for a good while.

It might have come to a head all at once, when she found out you were having an affair. She hates you. You've come to your senses, broken it off and realized what you have (or had). You want her. Bad. But the bridge is so burnt it appears impassable.

Or it might have been her affair that blew it up. Yes, she confessed to you. Yes, she broke it off and came crawling back. But can you ever trust her again? Can you ever love her the way you used to? She's "all-in" now, but can you "win her" so she never wanders off again?

Maybe it's over, but nobody's admitting it. You "grew apart." Her career has taken off . . . she's pouring more and more into her work, plus she's started taking courses at the community college and she's feeling "alive again." Maybe she's a stay-at-home mom who's decided she doesn't want to waste the years she has left doing your laundry and cooking your food. You've smothered her. She wants to breathe. Every day, there's more and more silence. Fewer friendly conversations. More anger. More frustration. Less patience. Less agreement — *on anything.*

So . . . how are you feeling? Uncertain? Uncomfortable? Overwhelmed? It's pretty hard for guys to step back and clearly see what's going on in their marriages. And it can be scary, even terrifying. But isn't it smarter to wade into your problems than to stick your head in the sand? Or run? Or get blindsided?

More big clues: You and your wife keep clashing over the same things . . .

Money. Why can't she see what she's doing to you? To the two of you. So much debt you can't breathe. No appreciation for how hard you're working. Never satisfied. Never grateful. No encouragement. Never enough.

Sex. Well, that's a sore subject. It's gotten less and less frequent. And more and more routine.

Friends. Yours are yours. Hers are hers. You don't trust hers. Your don't think they like you, and you're not sure they're good for your marriage. You wonder if they're advising her to leave you. You know yours are coaching you that way. *You're wasting your life, man, they say. Find somebody else. You guys just aren't happy. Get it over with and move on.*

The past. Your ex-wife. Her ex-husband. Something from the past "owns" you. She won't forgive you. You can't forgive her . . . or yourself. Either way, the past keeps coming back to steal the present. And paint a hopeless future.

Other people. There are some you don't want to disappoint — your parents, mentors and a few church friends. But most of your married friends will understand if you break up. They've seen things decline between the two of you. They want you to be happy, but wonder if you should stay married to each other.

Other women. Maybe that's where things have really fallen apart. You've met somebody who's everything your wife isn't. You may not have moved on it yet, but you've had enough conversations to be emotionally connected to her. You can't wait to get free so you can really hang out with her. It's going to be complicated, no doubt. But it's going to be worth it to finally be happy again.

Other men. You may be suspicious she's talking to someone else — or more than talking. She sure isn't talking to you. Nor is she the least bit interested in "physical" activities. She's cold as ice, but you know she's not a cold-as-ice woman. You just know there's no heat coming in your direction.

- **Boredom.** You love her (yes, you do), but it's the same old, same old. You're getting older. She's getting older. You look around and see no heroes in your world, nobody whose marriage you envy. You don't know what you want or what it will take, but you're tired of this and you're ready to do something else, even if it's wrong.

I don't know which of these you may be experiencing. Any one of them can cripple or even kill a marriage. You're feeling you need to do something, even if it's wrong.

On one hand, you've tried for a long time and you're tired. She's not going to change. She's all but told you that. She's showing little or no interest in anything you offer. She's written you off, either consciously or unconsciously.

On the other hand, you're not a quitter. What about the kids . . . your families . . . hers and yours? There's the hemorrhage of money a divorce will cost, not to mention child support for the rest of eternity. You have all this history with her, and it wasn't too bad at first. It's not like you totally hate her. You're just tired of the battle. Tired of the disappointment. Tired of the criticism. Tired of feeling like a stranger in your own house.

SO . . . WHATCHA GONNA DO?

If I had picked up this book 32 years ago, my response would have been, "adios." I'd have put this book away, put the whole deal out of my mind (again) and gone to bed. But 31 years ago, after it all "hit the fan," I'd have lapped up every word. Why? Because my world was turned upside down, and I didn't have a clue what to do. I realized I was in deep trouble, and I had to do something drastic if I was to save my marriage and find happiness. "Business as usual" was not going to cut it. I was disrupted. Seriously disrupted.

Since people don't buy solutions to problems they don't have, most of us won't change until we recognize a problem . . . until something or somebody turns up the heat. If you're not a little bit disrupted, a little bit shaken from your "homeostasis," you'll keep doing what you've always done and your marriage will stay where it is. My hope is you've read these snapshots and something's jacked you up! Whether out of fear or desire, you're ready to move. Ready to take responsibility and step up to win . . . and keep . . . your wife's heart.

It starts by going "on record" and letting her know that you're totally and irreversibly committed to her.

You may think it's silly.

But I'll bet she won't.

**STEP
ONE**

DECIDE AND TELL HER

*Decide you love your wife, that you want to spend the rest of
your life married to her, and then tell her — with downward
voice inflection — say it and mean it.*

kay, so this isn't all that exciting. But it's necessary. And it's
nonnegotiable. Everything else I'm going to suggest is useless if you
don't do this one.

Why?

Because your heart won't be in it.

In choosing to stay married, you're choosing a path that's long and hard, longer
and harder than any you've ever walked. You're going to be kicked in the groin,
ignored, screamed at, rejected and stonewalled. You're going to feel disrespected
and minimized as a man. Your needs are not only going to go unmet, they
are going to be ignored at times. There will be more setbacks than advances,
and it's not going to feel good most of the time. And if your marriage is at the
bottom, put your big-boy britches on, because it's not going to feel good for a
long time.

LET'S TALK ABOUT LOVE

As I said earlier, love is a choice you make . . . not a hole you fall into.

Yeah, when you got married, you loved your wife. You felt it. You were all pumped up and teary-eyed. We all are when we see her walking down the aisle, beautifully adorned in a gleaming white dress. Intense. No doubt about it.

But whether you feel it or not, you've got to choose to love your wife. And I'm not just talking about a day, a week or a month. I'm talking about *choosing* to love her *until you die*. You have to choose to be kind to her, no matter what she says or how she treats you. You have to choose to serve her, no matter how little she serves you. You have to *choose* to get into her frame of reference, regardless of the fact she never gets into yours. It's a one-way street with all the traffic headed in her direction and none headed back your way.

Are you up for that? Can you handle it? Are you willing to give love and not trade it?

I'm going to put wheels on what I mean in the chapters that follow. And I'm going to give you practical things to make your love for her come alive. And there's a chance, over time, she'll love you back and it won't always be a one-way street.

But if you're not willing to sign up for this kind of one-way commitment, your marriage won't ever be great. If you're already in trouble, your marriage won't make it.

LOVE VERSUS MARRIAGE

Marriage is easy when you're feeling the love. But when you aren't, marriage feels like a cage: *I'm trapped in here with this woman I don't love. And she doesn't love me. I can't get out and neither can she. This marriage is holding both of us back from being happy!*

We think marriage is the problem, that it's holding us back from someone or something better.

But think about this: *What if the cage is there to protect us?*

If you were deep in the jungles of Africa and there were hungry lions, tigers, leopards, jackals — all kinds of hungry animals looking for fresh meat — you'd give anything for a cage. You'd gladly lock yourself inside.

> **MAYBE THAT'S WHY WE HAVE MARRIAGE. MAYBE IT'S THERE TO PROTECT US FROM THE DANGERS … TEMPTATIONS WE'RE DRAWN TO … THINGS THAT WILL KILL US IF WE'RE SET FREE.**

Maybe that's why we have marriage. Maybe it's there to protect us from the dangers … temptations we're drawn to … things that will kill us if we're set free.

"SO WHAT" IF MARRIAGE *IS* AN "INSTITUTION"?

Think about why humans set up institutions. Institutions are set up to sustain important activities over time.

In years gone by, most small towns in the U.S. had a good-hearted doctor who took care of people in the community. When people were sick, he went to their homes and treated them. When they got really sick, he brought them to his house and looked after them until they got better or died.

What happened when the doctor died? Or when his house burned down? The whole community was out of luck.

So we created an *institution* to *sustain* the healthcare we all needed. The good-hearted doctor is still at the heart of it, but now connected to a hospital — an institution — a system that will carry on when he doesn't feel like being good-hearted, or when he's sick himself or when he's (ultimately) not around. Marriage is a system like that. It carries two people through when they don't feel love for each other. I say it this way . . .

Love *initiates* marriage. But *marriage* sustains love.

YOU HAVE TO DECIDE

It's like my friend Craig, who set out to run the Chicago Marathon. He decided he was going to finish no matter what. Sure, he wanted to finish in less than four hours, but his main deal was to finish.

It turned out to be "Chicago cold" the morning of the race. Undaunted, he set out on his mission. About eight miles in, he felt a weird pain in his calf. He kept running, albeit a little gingerly. At mile seventeen, he was in mortal agony. He kept running. At mile twenty-four, he was walking with a bad limp. When he crossed the finish line, he was dragging his bad leg and crying like a baby. But he finished.

That's the kind of commitment it takes to save a marriage or make one great. As leadership expert Andy Stanley says, "Somebody has to go first. By going first, the leader furnishes confidence to those who follow."[3] When you, the husband, lead with iron-clad commitment, you give confidence both to yourself and to your wife. But it has to be real. You have to make the long-term, irreversible decision — saying, "I'm all-in." And then *be* "all-in." Regardless.

A good friend of mine experienced what seems like the ultimate rejection for a man; his wife left him for a woman. He told me he was ready to hit the road and find someone else when we met for lunch. He was hurt big time, but he still loved her. I asked if he thought she would be open to meeting with me and he said yes. So I called her and, sure enough, she agreed to meet for lunch. Having a little bit of advance warning, I wasn't shocked when she revealed the nature of her extramarital affair. Actually, she was shocked I wasn't shocked.

I explained that who she had become involved with was irrelevant to the real question. "Did you mean it when you said, 'Till death do us part'?" I asked. I guess no one had confronted her that way, distracted by her gender choice more than her marriage vow. She got very emotional as I cast vision for what their kids' weddings would be like with multiple "moms" wearing expensive dresses and being escorted to the front. We talked for a long time, and she said she'd rethink what she was doing.

I got back with my friend and suggested he reach out to her. "If you love and accept her unconditionally, I think there's a chance she'll come back and recommit to you and your marriage. But if she doesn't, you can go to your grave knowing you never abandoned her or broke *your* commitment. If she breaks it, she breaks it. But you'll never have to apologize to your kids or feel like you didn't do everything you could possibly do. You'll feel good about yourself because you did the right thing."

But it was too late.

Not because her reflection came too late, but because her husband, my good friend, gave up. He broke *his* marriage commitment and found somebody else.

Divorce. Baggage. No redemption. Blended families. Multiple "moms."

Don't let that happen to you without a fight. Make a decision. Make a commitment. Grit your teeth and decide you're going to honor it and never quit. Never give up. If she leaves you, she'll leave the kindest, most attentive, most loving man in the world. But it'll be on her, not you.

YOU GOTTA TELL HER
One of my mentors taught me this . . .

"When people are telling you the truth, they telegraph it. When they don't mean what they say, they telegraph that too."

If you make the decision to love her no matter what, to *never* give up on your marriage, to be willing to look hard at yourself in the mirror and open up to becoming the man you want to be, that's huge. You need to tell her. But you have to tell her in the cool of the evening, not in the heat of the battle. You need to be together and face-to-face. You need to let her know what you're about to tell her is important . . . the genuine, from-the-heart, bone-level truth. Most importantly, you must tell her you're making this commitment for *yourself — for your benefit — not to win her heart.* That will blow her mind. But it has to be the truth.

You need to tell her you love her and won't ever leave, no matter what. She needs to hear from your mouth and your heart that you're *in . . . all in.* You're willing and ready to work on stuff, and you'll never give up on your marriage. And you must say it like you mean it because you mean it. A woman's need for security is near the top of her list. Your wife *wants to believe you love her and you'll never leave.* You owe it to her to decide, and then tell her.

AND NOTHING WILL CHANGE — FOR A WHILE

Let me be clear. When you make up your mind and commit to her and to your marriage forever, nothing is going to change, at least not at first. Maybe she'll ruin her mascara, but don't think these nice-sounding words are going to work magic. She knows you. She's heard stuff like this before. She may even call you out with, *Oh, you're going to give me that line again? No way I'm buying that hoo-hah! And if she does, don't try to sell her or convince her. Just smile gently and say, You'll see. I'm doing this for me. I'm committing to grow up and become the man I want to be. And I need your help. I need some time and a little slack. It won't take long for you to see my commitment is real.*

The most important part of making this decision and telling her isn't convincing *her.* It's being sure *yourself.*

WHY IT'S THE BEST DECISION

George Washington Carver once said, "Anything will give up its secrets if you love it enough."[4] Before he died, he patented 268 different uses for the peanut.

The peanut didn't love him back. But because of his intense, unwavering, life-long commitment to it, amazing things happened. Millions of people have peanut butter and jelly sandwiches every day. His one-way commitment changed the world. And your one-way commitment to your wife and marriage can change the world too, starting with yours, hers and your children's.

"No matter where you go, there you are." It's an old psychologist's joke, but it's true. If you think you're going to find someone who's better, who'll love you more, who'll be more like what you want, remember your next girl still has to fall in love and *stay in love with you*. If you're like me and most men I know, *that ain't no picnic*. Most people who divorce once are likely to divorce again — sometimes twice more. What's the common denominator? *They are.*

Committing to your wife and making your marriage work is by far the least expensive choice you have. Divorce, alimony and child support — they'll ultimately double your monthly expenses. You're going to feel more pressure to perform at work to make enough money to take care of everyone. That's a cage you don't want to be trapped in.

When you bail on your marriage, you give your kids permission to divorce when they get married. You can't tell them not to do something you did. You'll have no moral authority with your kids on the subject. You'll have punted, and you'll be completely discounted when it comes to the subject of commitment and staying with something even when it's hard.

THE CAR ANALOGY

Imagine the car you have today is the only car you can *ever* have.

I mean *ever.*

How would you treat that car? Would you take care of it? Would you invest in it, keep it serviced, and protect it from harm?

Would you abuse it? Take it for granted?

How much time would you spend looking at other men's cars online . . . or at new cars in the showroom?

Zero. None. Nada.

Because it would be a waste of time.

With no way to legitimately get another car, you'd learn to be content with yours. As a matter of fact, if you took care of it well enough, someday you could have a collector car that others would envy. Collector cars — really valuable ones — are cared for from the time they leave the showroom until they reach their ultimate destinations in museums. You may have already done damage to yours, but all that can be taken care of with time, effort and consistent "TLC."

So it is with your wife and your marriage.

If you'll commit to her forever, stop thinking about the woman you don't have, and give the one you have the time, warmth and love she needs, you might have a chance of pulling this thing out of the fire.

RADICAL HUSBANDS commit and stay committed.

BURN THE SHIPS

Eliminate all your escape routes. Whether they exist in your mind, on Facebook, in your address book or on the other side of town, you must seal off any open doors to other relationships. Your wife must become your only source of romance.

The second step on our list is to "burn the ships." You have to decide to eliminate any alternatives to your wife. This isn't a passive mental activity. It's active. It's actually *doing something* — *doing whatever it takes* to make your wife your only option, your only source of romance. Until she's the only one, you won't focus on her and do all the things you need to do. Until your wife is the only focus of your attention and romantic energy, you won't have any chance of winning her heart or keeping it over time. Rock promoter Bill Graham said of the Grateful Dead, "They're not the best at what they do, they're the only ones that do what they do."[5] It's called exclusivity.

The phrase "burn the ships" comes from the legendary story of Spanish Conquistador Hernando Cortez, who landed in Mexico in 1519 with a few hundred men, eleven ships, and plans to seize the great treasures of the Aztecs. Outnumbered by an army who'd turned back these kinds of conquests for six centuries, what would have to happen for Cortez to succeed where others had failed?

> **UNTIL YOUR WIFE IS THE ONLY FOCUS OF YOUR ATTENTION AND ROMANTIC ENERGY, YOU WON'T HAVE ANY CHANCE OF WINNING HER HEART OR KEEPING IT OVER TIME.**

Out of the blue, he uttered three words that changed everything.

"Burn the ships."

"*What? You gotta be kidding me*," his men probably thought.

"Burn the ships," he repeated.

Then he said this: "If we're going home, we're going home in their ships." With that, Cortez and his men burned their own ships. When the ships were toast, the alternative was removed. They were *committed*. It wasn't "win or go home." It was "win or you're never going home." That's different. There was no turning back. No alternative. No escape. No option other than to make it work.

All-in. 100-percent committed. Until-death-do-us-part committed.

If you want to win and keep her heart, you've got to burn your ships.

BIRTH OF A VISION

Human beings are smart. If there's anything built in us, it's the desire to survive. And to survive, we need hope. We need an alternative. A way out if all else fails.

When you said, "I do," this might have been far from your mind. Maybe not even there. You were so optimistic, so positive she was perfect. She would meet all your needs. Exceed your expectations.

But as reality "bit," you realized it wasn't that way. She's not perfect. She has a mind of her own. She wants to have her own life. She's not as crazy about you as she once was. She's not ready to have sex with you every time you want it.

So you conjure up alternatives in your mind. They're your second choices. Your escape routes. They're the grass that's greener. The DEFCON 5 alternative: *If she were to die, I'd probably* (fill in the blank).

These are men's ships. They're our way out if things really get tough. Or if she decides to bail, these are our fallback positions, our emergency landing strips. You may not think you have a ship, but if your marriage is in trouble, I'll bet you do. And things won't get better until you burn it. Eliminate it completely.

STANDARD OF COMPARISON

Author John Eldredge says men are born with questions burning in their souls: "Do I measure up? Do I have what it takes? Am I up to the task?"[6] These questions lie dormant throughout most of our childhood, but as soon as we become self-aware, as soon as we bump into our first bully or figure out there's a bigger kid in our grade who can run faster, jump higher or throw farther, we start comparing. It's just in us. The scratch golfer with the liquid swing, the guy with the $200,000 car, the beautiful woman in the low-cut dress on his arm. We want the best. We want what he has. We want it all or as close as we can get. *If I had someone like her . . . everyone would know that I have what it takes.* Without thinking about it, we've stitched together pictures of what we wish we had . . . of what would validate us. Those visions become our ships.

SO WHAT ARE YOUR SHIPS?

You can lie to everyone else, but try not to lie to yourself. Do you have a ship somewhere? Come on, be completely honest. When things are going okay, your ships sit in "dry dock" and get little thought or attention. But when a guy's marriage is in trouble, and he says, *There really isn't another woman*, I say he's usually lying. There is another woman. Whether she's real or imagined, there's a ship that beckons him, a ship that needs to be torched. Let's walk through the

> **. . . MEN'S SHIPS ARE OUR WAY OUT IF THINGS REALLY GET TOUGH.**

shipyard and figure out which one might belong to you.

THE LIFEBOAT

Some guys go into marriage leaving open the possibility of an affair or divorce from the get-go. *I'll do this because it seems like the thing to do right now. It'll please her. It'll please my mama. But there's no way I can know this is gonna work out. And there's no way I'm totally committing, not knowing the future. I'm keeping my options open.* One man I know said he went into marriage thinking: "Three years. . . . I'll give this three years. By then, it'll either work out or it won't." Another friend has always left the door open for an affair: "If this gets bad, I can always get 'supplemental love' on the side."

I think these are exceptions, but I can't prove it. It's hard to believe someone could go through the whole process of engagement, wedding, vows, ceremony . . . the whole she-bang . . . knowing they're lying, but these two confessed their half-heartedness to me personally. Both have come to see how having these "lifeboats" in the back of their minds kept them from experiencing real marriage. They were never really in the game until they burned their "lifeboats" and decided to go "all in" with one woman for all time.

THE OTHER WOMAN IN YOUR PRESENT

If a name has already flashed through your mind, then you have a ship that needs to be burned. The litmus test isn't whether you've slept with her or not. It's whether she has a name or not.

You see, marriage only works when it's exclusive. That means one woman is "in" and every other woman is "out." You can't share your love with anyone other than your wife. Period. A man can only love one woman at a time. If he divides his love, it dies for one and grows for another. Love is never stagnant — it either grows or dies. Always.

Here's a question, and it's a big one.

Does your "ship" know she's your "ship"? Does the other woman *know* she's the "other woman"?

This is a huge question you must answer honestly. Your answer drives what you must do to burn the ship. Other people's lives and marriages are at stake, so you've got to be straight here.

If she knows you care for her, whether you've slept with her or not, you have to **destroy** that relationship. You can't wait for your wife or her husband or anyone else to do it for you. And it can't be a pseudo-breakup. It has to be a real, burned-to-the-ground, no-hope-remains-for-this-relationship kind of destruction. And if your wife knows about it — even if she just suspects — she has to know you've burned it to the ground. She has to smell the smoke and see the ashes.

A young friend is walking through this right now. He let himself get emotionally involved with a woman he met at work and ended up having one of those "my wife doesn't really understand me" all-night conversations on a business trip. Problem is, his wife kept dialing his cell phone and, eventually, his hotel room. She figured out something was going on. Confronted, he confessed. All hell broke loose and she moved out. Then she moved back in and made him move out.

Twelve weeks later, through a lot of honesty, forgiveness and counseling, she invited him to move back in. The night before he was to unpack his suitcase, he left his iPad for the kids to watch movies. His wife decided to scroll through his emails and BAM! — she found emails between his "friend" and him. They were months old, but they busted the stitches and started the bleeding again.

My advice to him?

> "Write your friend a ***final*** email. Tell her that you've made a permanent, irreversible decision to end your relationship AND your friendship. Tell

her you love your wife and family with all your heart and you'll never look her way again. Ever. Show the email to your wife, and if she wants to help you craft the words, let her. The goal is to burn the ship, to scorch the earth so you can't ever go back there. If your wife has words that'll help you, use them. Send the email. Then delete the address from your address book and delete every email from your history. Make her be gone. Erased. From here forward — nonexistent.

If she works where you work, start looking for another job. Your marriage and family hang in the balance. You can't trust yourself to never return to the ship. The ship has to be gone. It can't just be hard to go back. It has to be impossible to go back, at least in your mind's eye. And in your wife's.

While your concern isn't for the other woman, you've served her well by burning the ship. She now has clarity. You're not an option. Maybe she'll put her energy into her marriage or into finding a meaningful relationship with someone other than another woman's husband."

Strong stuff. You're going to need balls to do what RADICAL HUSBANDS do.

THE OTHER WOMAN FROM YOUR PAST

A friend of a friend reconnected with his high school sweetheart via Facebook. The conversation moved from the Internet to a coffee shop to a hotel to a divorce. This other woman had been in his mind for all the years of his marriage. She didn't know it — until he saw her Facebook page and asked her to be "friends."

Someone else I know had a high school sweetheart. There was no sex involved. It was a normal, healthy little dating relationship as kids back in the '60s. Eventually, they broke up and went their separate ways. But the guy never forgot this girl. In his mind, she was the *ultimate*, the one who got away. And she kept him in the same spot in her imagination. Years later, when both had been married for more than a decade, their marriages were in trouble. Where did they turn? To each other. And it didn't take them long. They had lived separate lives. Moved to different places. Had kids and built families. And they'd considered themselves friends. He'd call her on her birthday just to say hello. Totally innocent. Completely platonic.

Legally, relationally, rationally . . . maybe even spiritually . . . there was nothing there. But psychologically, there was a vision. There was an imaginary wife who would have been perfect in every way. No woman could ever trump her, because she didn't exist in reality, only in his mind. Neither of them felt like they had "settled for less" when they first got married. The relationship was in the distant past.

But as things got rocky in their marriages, memories of the old flame came alive. Vivid minds and broken hearts took what was black and white and made it full color. Technicolor. None of the faults were there. Neither of them could remember why they broke up way back then. It was all kindness, perfume and roses. *She was the right one for me. He'd have loved me the way I wanted to be loved.* Legends in their minds.

Who can compete with a vision? How can you "win" when the alternative exists in someone's imagination? Never messes up? Never has bad breath? Never disappoints?

Imagine how it feels to be that guy's wife. You can never quite get it right. Never quite be lovely or lovable enough. No matter what she does or how hard she tries, there's a sense she's being judged, being compared to perfection. Never mind that "perfection" doesn't exist.

Is that guy you?

Is there someone like that running around in your mind? Have you built the perfect imaginary wife from memories of someone from your past? Do you look at her Facebook page? Still hold on to a phone number? Picture? Mailing address?

You've got to burn the ship.

THE NAMELESS OTHER WOMAN IN YOUR MIND

You may be thinking, *I'm off the hook. I don't have a real-time other woman. And there's nobody from my past I'm thinking about.*

But for most men, there's probably another woman hanging out there in their memory or imagination. You didn't go into marriage with a "lifeboat," but you've developed one since. In your mind, there's a better deal. There's got to be.

Everywhere we look, we see beautiful women. Turn on network television, anytime. Turn on a ball game — any kind of ball game — and within minutes, you'll see beautiful women dancing seductively with beer in their hands. Short skirts. Big boobs. Cleavage everywhere. Just waiting for you. Movies? Same. Magazines? Same. Websites? Same. And around the office? Eye candy left and right. On the street? In the grocery store? Unavoidable. Today's fashions, diets, plastic surgeries and the absence of modesty have created an R-rated world for guys. We don't get a choice. Sexy women are everywhere.

But the big one, the overwhelming thing that's creating the "other woman" in men's minds, is porn. Eighty-six percent of American men between 18 and 26 years old have used porn in the last year[7]. It's rampant. I just want to talk about what happens when we look at it. How our minds create imaginary ships, ships our wives can never compete with. Ships that change from imaginary to real . . . as real as divorce papers. Here's how it happens.

FOUR STAGES OF SHIP CONSTRUCTION

STAGE ONE: INNOCENT SNAPSHOT

Unless you're blind, you're going to see beautiful, sexy women. She's going to open her car door and swing her legs out. Her short skirt's going to leave little to your imagination. You're going to be watching

TV when a Victoria's Secret commercial comes on. Before you know it, you're going to see bras and thongs. You're looking for something on the Web and BAM! — there's an image you didn't ask for. Or maybe you did.

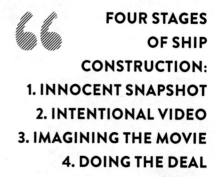

FOUR STAGES OF SHIP CONSTRUCTION:
1. INNOCENT SNAPSHOT
2. INTENTIONAL VIDEO
3. IMAGINING THE MOVIE
4. DOING THE DEAL

Your ship is pretty easy to burn at this stage. Just look away and move on. You haven't done anything wrong. You haven't used any of your emotional or romantic energy. You saw something, but you didn't focus on it. You looked away and didn't linger. You're clean.

STAGE TWO: INTENTIONAL VIDEO

Let's say you don't look away. You keep looking. You watch the whole Victoria's Secret commercial. Or the whole show. You watch the girl in the short skirt get out of the car, and you even walk behind her into the grocery store, checking her out as she walks in and takes her cart. Or you linger on the website and click to a second page. Then a third. You hover.

Now burning the ship becomes a little harder. You feel guilty because you intentionally took the next step. You did something to keep looking. But you can still easily opt out. You decide, *Okay, that's enough. This isn't good for me. I'm done with this.* You've gone beyond innocence, but you opted out before you got to the next stage — imagination.

STAGE THREE: IMAGINING THE MOVIE

If you stay focused on these images, you're moving in deeper. Let's say you get your cart and stroll around the grocery store, watching the short skirt, imagining what it would be like if she came over and said: *Hey, my husband's out of town. Would you come over and help me unload my groceries?* Or you close your eyes after the Victoria's Secret commercial. You visualize that beautiful young woman dancing in your bedroom. Or you stay on the porn site and watch the action, imagining you're the guy in the movie. Now you feel dirty. You took what was innocent . . . a glance at a woman on the produce aisle . . . and intentionally made more of it than it had to be. Then you went further, imagining yourself doing things with a woman who isn't your wife. You're building a ship.

When you look at women, especially on porn sites, you start building expectations for your wife. You start constructing a standard for what a woman should look like and what she should do in bed. In reality, that woman doesn't exist. The producers of porn create those images in studios with actors and actresses, lighting and makeup. They do takes and retakes. They make it as real as the Titanic in James Cameron's film. Problem is, Cameron's Titanic didn't really exist. It was fake — created for the movie. And so is that woman you see on your computer screen. She only exists in your head, in your mind's eye.

It's a lot harder to opt out now. You've created an imaginary ship, and it's one you can go back to. Whenever you go to the grocery store, you relive your imaginary encounter. You can go back to the imaginary woman you made love to on the Web. You've created another life in your mind and there's this beautiful woman in it with you. She's not your wife. She's younger. Fresher. More beautiful. And she never complains. Your wife doesn't know she exists, but she's there constantly — in your head. You're emotionally engaged with someone other than your wife. Your wife is doomed to failure, being constantly compared with a perfect figment of your imagination. You've abandoned your wife.

Do you see? You're wasting energy you could be spending on your wife. On the real woman in your life. Do you sense the abyss you're pouring your mental and emotional energy into?

But if you burn the ship now, you can avoid the pain that comes with the final stage.

STAGE FOUR: DOING THE DEAL

Simply stated, you put skin on the woman you imagined. You find a ship you can actually board. Yeah, she doesn't look *exactly* like the women you watched on your computer. But by now, you've cut your wife down so low in comparison, anybody's better than her. You're wide open to any willing woman who offers hope of being what your mind created. Opting out now is nearly impossible. Your ship now has a name. Burning it is going to be painful, with consequences. But it has to happen, and it has to be final.

BETWEEN YOUR EARS

Golf legend Bobby Jones said, "The game of golf is played mainly on a five-inch course, in a space between your ears."[8] Marriage is similar. It requires exclusive and singular focus on one woman.

If you're to win and keep your wife's heart, you've got to burn the ships. With names, with skin, from the past, in your imagination — all of them. You've got to start bouncing your eyes and turning your mind away from anyone who can distract you from the single legitimate source of romance you'll ever have in this lifetime.

ONE MORE SHIP: YOU

Now you say, *I am off the hook. I don't have another woman. Not in reality. Not in my mind. Not on the Internet. None.*

You may be one of those guys (and I know a few of them) with the genetic makeup that makes it easy for them to be "one-woman men." Swedish researchers looked at variants of a particular gene — the "monogamy gene" — that encodes a hormone called vasopressin. They found that one of these variants (or a lack thereof) is associated with a distinctive kind of pair-bonding behavior in men. The findings suggest an explanation for why some men commit to monogamous relationships while others have a hard time shaking their frat-house habits.[9]

Lucky you. But you're not devoid of ships.

Your ship may be your work. Or ESPN. Or golf. Or college football. Or the kids' sports teams you coach. Your ship is anything you engage with that *owns* you. Sucks all your emotional energy into it and away from your wife.

If you're going to be a RADICAL HUSBAND, you have to burn the ship. You have to make your wife your *single source of romance*, your marriage the *primary* focus of your attention and energy.

Sounds tough doesn't it?

It is, but it's worth it.

THREE

DROP YOUR EXPECTATIONS

You've created expectations for your wife. Not only has she not met them;
she's done with trying. Done with feeling like a failure. Your only hope is
to drop your expectations . . . all of them . . . and love her just as she is.

For the next few pages, I want to speak to the guy whose marriage is in trouble. (The rest of you might want to listen in.)

Let me start with a little confession.

After our first twelve years of marriage, I was done. I was convinced I had married the wrong woman. She wasn't romantic; she wasn't spontaneous; she wasn't any fun; she didn't want to go anywhere or do anything. All she cared about were the kids and how the house was decorated. We had "grown apart," as they say.

I was working a lot of hours, traveling a good bit and had lots of time around professional women who seemed to have it going on. 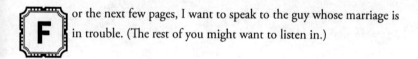 *My fear*

I wanted to fix Miriam, so I suggested we go to a marriage counselor. I'll never forget parading my wife in there like a broken-down Ferrari. "Here," I was going to say, "help her see the error of her ways and get her on track."

It was awful.

The counselor saw my selfishness as clearly as a big, smushed bug in the middle of a windshield. She started asking me questions like the ones I asked you a few minutes ago. I was humiliated — *embarrassed beyond belief.* I was humbled, to say the least.

Even though I "heard" the truth about what I was doing, it took Miriam leaving me a week later for me to get it, to feel it, to realize I was in a death knell of selfish expectations that was killing her love and our marriage. Only in the solitude of a house without my wife, with no promise of her coming back — ever — only then did I face myself and decide I had to change.

IF YOU'RE LIKE ME . . .

. . . you've put expectations on your wife, and she didn't meet them. They didn't seem all that bad at the time. You probably didn't even realize you were doing it. But little by little, you created a win-lose situation. If she did what you expected, you were happy — at least not unhappy. But if she didn't measure up, you weren't happy and you let her know. Sometimes verbally. Usually nonverbally. The silent treatment. The smirk. The roll of your eyes. The look down or away. She's smart, and she's sensitive. She knows when she doesn't measure up. Believe it or not, she wants to. Or wanted to, but never quite could. After a while, she gave up.

Oh, your expectations are totally justified in your mind's eye. *Why shouldn't a guy come home to a "refuge"?* Your mama didn't expect your daddy to help her in the kitchen or play with the kids when he came home. He came home, fixed a drink for himself, sat down in his recliner and watched TV till dinner was ready. And so what if your mama didn't work outside the home? *The roles are still the roles!*

Really?

You think: *What's up with all this mess around the house? Why can't she get her act together and keep things neat? She has all day.* It seems she could organize her time better and get stuff done. She's got time to talk to her mama, her sister and all those girlfriends. But she can't find time to pick the clothes up off the floor or get the spoiled groceries out of the refrigerator. Every time you look out a dirty window, you think how much better she could be.

You love to hang out with friends and stuff. She knows that, but it takes an act of Congress for the two of you to go out. She talks about not being able to find a babysitter. She talks about not having anything to wear. She talks about being tired. You hear complaining. She's telling you how she feels . . . that she'd rather go out with just the two of you or stay at home together. What happened to the dancin' girl who wanted to party? Where's the girl you fell in love with?

Or maybe it's the reverse. She wants to go out with her friends and their husbands, to get dressed up and spend a bunch of money on a fancy dinner. You'd rather stay home, watch a ball game and just hang out. That's not in her vocabulary anymore. She never seems to want to do what you want to do.

Speaking of love and things that are missing, what happened to your love life? Where's the "spunky monkey" who wore you out for the entire first year of your marriage? Now it's a tug-of-war to get her in bed. She wants things her way and only her way. So routine. Not bad, but routine. And so predictable, so infrequent, so more out of duty than passion.

A lot of the time, she's not even willing to hit the sack in the same time zone with you. You eat dinner, stick around till the kids are down, check email and get a little work done. By the time you're finished, she's fast asleep. If you skip the work and get to bed earlier, she's up doing chores or watching some inane TV show you have no interest in.

You remember when she used to dress up. I mean, she looked like a fashion model. She's let herself go, never lost those pregnancy pounds. She doesn't dress like she used to. You used to get pretty pumped just looking at her. Now she looks pretty much like every other woman in the carpool line.

Then there's her family. You'd think you never got married. She wants to go to her mother's for every freakin' holiday. It would seem by now we'd be a family, and she'd be satisfied being here. And your family . . . they're all werewolves. She has no interest or energy for them whatsoever.

You love your kids just as much as she does. In fact, you'd die for them. But they are **all** she cares about. All she thinks about. All she wants to talk about. There's never any bandwidth for you, for "us." It's all about the kids.

And then there's money. You work your butt off to provide; maybe you both do. But when it comes to spending, she just doesn't make wise choices. *How many chocolate bunnies do you need to make a good Easter basket? Are we dressing the kids for the playground or a magazine shoot? And do we have to have "organic" toilet paper?* Come on!

HAVE YOU BUILT A CASE AGAINST YOUR WIFE?
Little by little, you've built your case: *She didn't do that. She's not like this anymore. If she'd only be like this other woman I know at work.*

Now hear this . . .

Anxiety comes from unmet expectations.

Let me say it again. I'm saying it louder this time . . .

Anxiety comes from unmet expectations!

Your anxiety about your wife and marriage is coming from *your* unmet expectations.

Right now, you may have a ton of anxiety. This isn't what you signed up for. Your anxiety has turned to anger. Your expectations have become demands. You've become impatient, intolerant and less loving. Your words and demeanor have become downright mean.

People use anger to justify doing what they want to do. To give themselves permission to do bad stuff. You (or she) may have justified some really stupid decisions by blaming your anger: *Since **you** care so little about me and my needs, I'll go find someone who will. Anger towards a person says, You owe me, and since I'm owed and you're not in the mood to pay me, I'll find someone or something that will.* You've given yourself permission to do stuff that can blow up your marriage, all because your wife isn't meeting the expectations you created for her. Expectations she may or may not even know about.

So here are a few questions for you:
- What gives you the right to decide what another person should or shouldn't do?
- What gives you the authority to set up pass/fail standards for your wife?
- Just where did you get the idea that your vision of what she's supposed to do, or to be like, is right?

HOW DO I HOPE YOU FEEL RIGHT NOW?
Like a piece of "you-know-what"!

If that's how you feel, there's hope. If you don't, you may be beyond repair, at least right now. If your response to this rant is, *That's not me*, or *So what's wrong with that?* or any other response that starts with, *But what about* . . . or *I think I deserve* . . . it's game over, and you're not ready to be a RADICAL HUSBAND. Put this book away and get it back out when you've been humbled and broken, either through the end of this marriage or a future one.

On second thought, keep reading. The answers are right here in this book if you'll just grab these steps and go with them.

THE PAINFUL, PRODUCTIVE ANSWER

I wish there were an easier way. I really do. But there's not.

You have to drop your expectations. Eliminate them. Completely.

Expectations are the enemy of intimacy. Stop putting expectations on your wife and watch things change. It'll blow you away. You have to decide that you're going to accept your wife just as she is, regardless of how you wish she were. It's a decision you'll make and make and make. You'll get it right once. Then you'll get it wrong twice. You'll ask forgiveness. Then you'll screw up and have to ask forgiveness again.

So repeat the "Happy Wife Pledge" after me:

My wife is more important than the house being messy. I will shut up and start helping out.

My working wife is my partner in life. I will collaborate with her in consistent respect for her wants and needs.

I will no longer criticize my wife about how she uses her time. It's her life to live.

I am grateful for a wife who cares about our kids. I will thank her and encourage her, never allowing myself to be jealous again.

I recognize that my wife was her mom's daughter before she was my wife. She has a right and a responsibility to be a good adult daughter and to honor her mother.

I will never again complain about the food in our house. Instead, I will offer to stop by the store and bring whatever we need without complaint.

I will never criticize my wife for her desire to be "just with me" versus going out with friends. I will thank her and pour myself into loving her when we're together.

I recognize that my wife gets tired. I will drop all my demands and make "space" for her to rest, and I will not take it personally. ✓

I acknowledge that it is difficult to identify, screen and coordinate schedules with babysitters. I will not criticize her or take her efforts for granted.

I will look for the good in my wife's appearance. If I can't say something nice, I will keep my mouth shut.

I will never again comment on my wife's weight. That is off-limits to me forever. I will love and accept her regardless. It is none of my business.

I will never say anything negative about my wife, even in a joking way, in front of any other person, male or female, friend or foe. ✓

I will never bring up my wife's performance in earlier parts of her life. For example, I will never talk about how "she used to like to dance" or anything of that nature.

I will stop talking about sex. I will make no other comments, jokes, side comments or criticisms about the frequency, quality or any other dimension of our sex life. I will love her, and we will enjoy sex only when she is clearly in favor of it. I will put her first, be grateful for what comes my way and be content.

I recognize that my family of origin is just that — my family. I will drop my expectations for my wife to engage with my family. I hope she does, but I will not require it of her.

I will go through a complete review of our finances. I will make sure she fully understands our income, our budgeted expenses, our saving and giving commitments. And I will never again criticize her regarding money. ✓

As you look at this list of pledges, can you see the expectations you've been putting on your wife? Can you grasp the relief she'll feel when you promise to do all these things and you actually do them? Can you sense the walls that will come down when you actually stop demanding things and criticizing her?

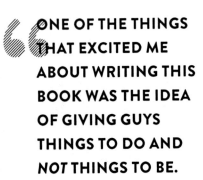

ONE OF THE THINGS THAT EXCITED ME ABOUT WRITING THIS BOOK WAS THE IDEA OF GIVING GUYS THINGS TO DO AND *NOT* THINGS TO BE.

BUT I'M NOT IN TROUBLE!

If I were a betting man, I'd wager the more of these pledge statements you live out, the closer your marriage is to being great. Even where things are just okay, you'll find guys who make fewer demands . . . guys who are a bit more "live and let live." But I don't want you miss out on the upside that can come from holding back on the expectations altogether.

Think about it. Who wouldn't want to be married to a guy who is sensitive and selfless?

Make these pledges, live them out and watch what happens. I predict you'll see your marriage transformed before your very eyes. And in less time than you'd imagine.

One of the things that excited me about writing this book was the idea of giving guys *things to do* and ***not** things to be*. It's really hard to change yourself and impossible to change someone else. But if you work at it, you can "move the needle" by not putting expectations on your wife.

Start with this. Listen to your words and thoughts. Start paying attention to what you're thinking and saying . . . words that subtly communicate an expectation . . . one that wasn't met or one you expect to be met in the future. The mind is sneaky. You'll hear yourself thinking (and saying) things like:

I know you're not excited about going to the ballgame next weekend, but I sure hope you decide to go.

I noticed you added a few things to that online order. Didn't we talk about that?

*It **is** date night, and I can't wait to get you home!*

Frank's wife really loves to dance. Do you think we could dance a few times tonight?

Behind every one of these questions or statements is an expectation. Behind every single one is the opportunity for your wife to fail. Do you think she doesn't know what you're really saying (or asking) with each of these statements or questions?

For the next week, wrestle your tongue to the bottom of your mouth and shut up. Listen for these kinds of statements and questions and arrest them **before** you say them. Your wife knows what you want…she knows what you expect. Give her a chance to speak and act on her own. You might be surprised just how many times she moves in your direction. And if she doesn't, she doesn't. She has that right. It's up to you to warm her heart toward you so she'll want to do some of the things you want to do. But you'll never know what she'll do, if you can't hold your tongue and keep setting her up on pass/fail.

DON'T SOLVE PROBLEMS, SET GOALS

This step might have been too much. Too familiar. Scary to think about what you've been putting on your wife. Intimidating to think what it'll take to stop. But like the old Chinese proverb says, "A journey of a thousand miles begins with a single step." The first step here is holding your tongue and overhauling your attitude.

That's what it's going to take — a complete overhaul of you when it comes to your expectations. You're going to have to learn to accept her as she is . . . to accept what she does . . . and to be content.

We've all heard, "Don't sweat the small stuff." Well, it's all small stuff. In the context of life . . . compared to the significance of divorce, a broken home, latchkey kids and multiple mamas at weddings . . . it's all small stuff.

You can do this. RADICAL HUSBANDS drop their expectations.

STEP
FOUR

LOVE WHAT
SHE LOVES

*Your wife's heart is warmed when she sees you loving
what she loves. It can't be fake or manipulative.
It has to be real and sustained.*

There's a chance if you're reading this, your wife may not be all that jazzed when she looks at you. She may see her biggest critic. You may remind her of all the cut-downs, the insensitivity and hurt you've brought her over the years. Certainly, trying to talk her into liking you isn't going to do the trick. When she hears your voice, it may echo your harsh, careless words. Or the sense she has from childhood of not being "lovable."

When Miriam finally, called a week after she left, I started telling her about all the changes I'd made and how much better I was going to be if she'd give me another chance. She wasn't buying it.

But she decided to come back. As the days and weeks went by, I became very intentional as a father. As I "turned a new leaf" and began trying to be a better man, I truly engaged with our kids. Oh, I'd been at all their games and recitals; all their school plays and practices. But before, I'd been going through the motions. My body had been there, but my mind was always on other stuff, primarily on my job and career. Now, I was **there**. I was focused, engaged and truly paying attention. I was appreciating their young personalities. I was observing their interactions with their classmates, teammates and friends. I was listening to how they interacted with their teachers, coaches and adults. I was focused on being thoughtful and kind in every single interaction with them. After all, I'd just come to the startling realization that they might be moving out of town with their mother . . . that I was very close to becoming an every-other-weekend dad.

I had also begun to commit to things that brought me more "into their world." I agreed to be a Cub Scout leader. Me — a Cub Scout leader! I had been so cynical about those "losers who had nothing better to do than to teach snotty-nosed, eight-year-olds how to tie knots and build fires." Now I was wearing a khaki shirt with patches all over baking a cake with my son.

BAKING A CAKE AND MAKING A COMEBACK

As we were destroying her kitchen . . . as I was trying something I had *never done nor appreciated before* . . . I noticed something. Out of the corner of my eye, I saw Miriam watching me. She didn't say anything, but I could see a faint smile on her face. She was digging what she was seeing. She loved seeing the father of her kids loving her kids. A bell rang for me, and I've never forgotten it:

> **If you want someone to love you, love what they love — especially their kids.**

I had always loved my kids, so I wasn't faking anything. But I had let my selfishness, and particularly my career, get way out of control and take me far, far away from what was really important. Now I was back. With Miriam seeing me working closely with our son, flour everywhere, figuring out ingredients and mixing up stuff, she caught a glimpse of the man I might become. If only for a moment, she saw something she liked.

STUDY YOUR WIFE

Maybe your next problem is that you don't know what she loves. Most of the men I know couldn't list more than three or four things their wives love — truly love. So you may have a lot of work to do in getting to know your wife.

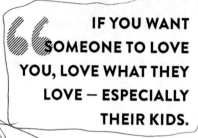

> IF YOU WANT SOMEONE TO LOVE YOU, LOVE WHAT THEY LOVE — ESPECIALLY THEIR KIDS.

So let's take the easy one first.

You know she loves her kids. I know, I know, you do too. But she loves them in a different way. She carried them around in her belly for nine months before they painfully squeezed out of her body. She has a connection that's different from yours. And she loves them in a way you don't.

Analyze that. Think about things she does with her kids. For her kids. Think about how you can begin to love those kids in some of the same ways she does. She probably doesn't "love" them by buying them candy or toys, which is the way most of us guys think. She has her ways . . . ways you can learn from.

A lot of moms show love to their kids by cooking meals for them, by helping them with their homework or helping them understand their friends and what's going on in those relationships. You can do that too, if you'll take the time.

Where we live, it seems that moms carry most of the carpool duties. It doesn't have to be that way. You can volunteer to take or pick up kids from school or after-school activities. Your wife can see you becoming more engaged with her kids . . . more and more available. She's going to like that.

If you're a blended family, there could be kids you didn't "father" but that she loves with all her heart. These kids might be part of the reason you've got so many problems. But if you were to start to love them intentionally, you'd probably see a change in her attitude. You can't replace their biological dad . . . I'm not suggesting that. But anytime you love what she loves, you warm her heart.

With women, their offspring (their children) is a class unto itself. Everything else is secondary. You know your wife better than anybody. You may have neglected her loves, you may have ignored what she cares about, but you probably still know, if you think about it.

Take a few minutes and write down what your wife loves.

Do it now.

Take your time.

This is important.

I'm going on a little rant of things wives sometimes love. This is just to get you started if you're stuck . . .

- *Animals. Dogs, cats and horses.* If she has one (or more) of these, you can decide that you're going to love it (them). It's an act of the will, I know. But God made 'em. He loves you, so you can love them — if you'll try.

- *Mothers.* Most women love their mothers big time, in a way that's special (see note about birthing babies above). If you'll bury the past and bury the hatchet with your mother-in-law, you might just find she's a person who never meant you any harm. If you can change your heart toward her and start to love and serve her a little, you might just find your wife more amenable to connecting with you.

- *Television.* Going out on a limb here, but if your wife really loves a particular show, watch it with her. Keep your critical mouth shut and watch it — the whole thing. There's something positive in everything. Look for it.

- *Hobbies, sports and activities.* Take a new look at the things she loves to do. Humble yourself and give them another try. Talk to her about them. Be honest and real. Ask for her help and advice. You might find you genuinely like something she loves. And if she sees you give it an honest try, you can't lose.

- ✓ *Books.* A wise friend once said, "Marry someone who's read the same books as you." Men who read find it easy to criticize, discount and write off the books their wives read. When you lean into a book that your wife loves and you find that you love it too, the principle kicks in — *when she sees you love what she loves, her heart will warm up to you.*

  MUSIC

- *Home.* The place you live. If you become a little more involved in making your home into the place your wife visualizes it to be, you might be surprised at her response. The more interest you take in home . . . the more you get into her frame of reference and stop battling against her vision of home . . . the more likely it is she'll warm up.

- *Work.* If your wife works outside the home, get interested in her job. Not to pry, not to give advice or try to "fix" anything, just to express genuine interest where she spends large chunks of time and energy. Express more than a passing interest in her work, her coworkers, her stresses and her dreams.

Gordon McDonald writes about how great his wife was about giving him critique on the sermons he preached. If he screwed up really bad, he'd know it right away. He could see it as it was happening by the lack of response from the audience. She'd know it too, but she'd stay quiet. She knew how much he loved developing those sermons, how hard he worked to make them perfect, how much it hurt when a sermon didn't "work." After a few days, he'd talk with her about it, and she'd gently give him an idea or two about what he might have done to make it better.

One day he came home and there was a real estate flyer with a picture of a house in a city 2,000 miles away. She'd left a note saying, "I want to live in this house!" When she came in later, he asked about the curious note about the far-away house. "We can't move there. That's crazy. My job is here. This is where we live. What are you trying to say?" he blustered.

Then she nailed him. "I've been trying to tell you how much I want to remodel and add that side porch. You brush me off, ignore me and make me feel foolish for even wanting it. When I saw this picture of a house with the porch just like I want, I thought, 'Maybe he'll understand if I put it this way!' "

McDonald netted it out this way: "My wife's house is *her sermon*. I owe her the same interest in her stuff that she shows in mine."[10]

WHEN ALL ELSE FAILS

If you've been as sorry a husband as I was for the first 12 years of my marriage, you don't have a clue about what your wife actually loves, except maybe her kids and her mom. You probably know more about what some of your co-workers love than your wife.

So you're going to have to find out. If you ask directly, she's going to suspect you're trying to manipulate her, and she's not going to buy into that. You're going to have to have real conversations. You're going to have to ask open-ended questions. You're going to have to really listen and make mental notes. You're going to have to start doing some of the things you should have been doing all along — because if you had, you might find your marriage in a better place.

The bottom line?

RADICAL HUSBANDS put away their selfishness and figure out what their wives love. Then they love it too.

STEP
FIVE

CREATE AN ENVIRONMENT OF ACCEPTANCE

---

*Your wife will gravitate toward an environment of **acceptance** and **away** from an environment of **rejection** and **criticism**.*

People can't change other people. Period. You can't change how another person thinks or what one believes. And you certainly can't change how another person feels. All you can do is create an environment that will feel different, and hopefully . . . maybe, someday . . . they will.

Let's start at the beginning.

ACCEPTANCE 101

The word "love" gets batted around everywhere. It's easy to say, "I love people." "I love everybody." "I love my wife." Even, "I love you."

And maybe you do.

But do you accept people? Do you accept *everybody*? Do you accept your wife?

There's a difference. A big difference.

Love is a big, amorphous word that has multiple meanings. You can love a serial killer, meaning you wouldn't want him to be given a death sentence. You can love poor African kids — even sponsor them with a monthly donation — but would you truly accept them if they lived next door? Just like they are? Messy? Smelly? Sick? Loud? Begging and stealing to eat and stay alive?

Let me bring it closer to home with a more practical illustration.

A former professional football player has two sons. One grows up to be a great high school quarterback. The kid's phenomenal. He's just like his dad: gregarious, good- looking, buff and recruited by all the best schools.

The other son is overweight and loves music. He's an introvert. For whatever reason, he's developed what looks to be a terminal case of acne. His few friends are all "geeks." They play video games constantly.

The dad *loves* both his sons. But which will be easier to *accept*?

It's often harder to accept someone than it is to love them. Acceptance isn't positional. The football player has to love both his sons because they're his sons. But he doesn't have to accept them. He can criticize, ignore, reject, minimize and even make jokes about his non-athletic son and still love him. He can create an environment of rejection without realizing he's doing it.

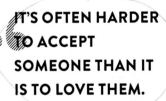

IT'S OFTEN HARDER TO ACCEPT SOMEONE THAN IT IS TO LOVE THEM.

Sometimes that's what we do to our wives.

Little by little, she was just "wrong." Everything about her. The house is *wrong* when you come home. She handles the kids *wrong*. She looks *wrong*. Her clothes are *wrong*. Her size is *wrong*. The decisions she makes are *wrong*. Her friends are *wrong*. How she spends her time is *wrong*. She's just *wrong, wrong, wrong*.

It's possible that you haven't said any of this aloud, but maybe you've thought it. And you've communicated it to her. She doesn't feel accepted; she feels rejected. And whenever you're together, no matter where it is, that's how she feels.

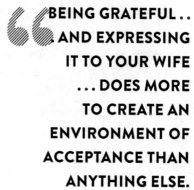

> BEING GRATEFUL... AND EXPRESSING IT TO YOUR WIFE ... DOES MORE TO CREATE AN ENVIRONMENT OF ACCEPTANCE THAN ANYTHING ELSE.

So how do you create an environment of acceptance?

EXPRESS GRATITUDE

Being grateful . . . and expressing it to your wife . . . does more to create an environment of acceptance than anything else. Who doesn't want to be appreciated? She committed *her life* to you — *her one and only life* on this earth, and she committed to spend it with you! That in itself deserves a deep and consistent word of gratitude.

Start thinking about who she is . . . her character qualities. Every single one of them is something to be grateful for. If you don't believe it, just flip 'em around and look at the opposites. Imagine what your wife (and your life) would be like if she were _____ instead of _____.

One of the assignments I give the younger men I mentor is to make a list of the 10 things they most admire about their wives. Not physical characteristics . . . being pretty or tall isn't something they had any control over. But character qualities . . . things that define who they are. Their personalities, the ways they interact with others. Here are some examples of things men admire about their wives.

I admire my wife's patience, especially with our children.
I admire the way my wife spends money carefully. She is frugal.
I admire the way my wife listens to people and shows she cares.
I admire my wife's taste in clothes. She makes good fashion decisions.
I admire my wife's faith. She's never rattled in a crisis.
I admire the way my wife stands up for me with other people.
I admire the way my wife serves her aging parents. She's a great daughter.
I admire my wife's kindness to animals. Our kids want to be like her.
I admire how organized my wife is. Nothing in our house falls through the cracks.
I admire the way my wife loves her friends. She loves and serves them so well.

If you're thinking, *None of that's true about my wife,* then go back to Step 3. If you're focused on making things better, turn away from what's not (or what you can't see right now), and turn toward her redeeming qualities.

TRY IT!

Sit down right now and make a list of the things that are great about your wife. What do you admire about her? What drew you to her in the first place? What would you say about her at her funeral?

Think long and hard about this. When you're done, consider asking her out on a special date and going over it with her. It has to be heartfelt; it can't be just another trick to get in her good graces. She'll see through that. Even if you give it to her, keep a copy somewhere you'll see it regularly. Put it in your underwear drawer. Read one of those qualities each day. Keep focused on what you love about her, one thing at a time, and your appreciation for her will grow and start to overflow into acceptance.

It's a different deal to express gratitude for *who someone is* versus what he or she *does.* We're all numb to the *Thanks for picking up my laundry,* or *I appreciate you letting me sleep in this morning.* Good things, yes, but those comments don't resonate in the soul like: *You have the kindest heart of anyone I know. When I watched you stop and talk to that old man in the wheelchair, I remembered why I've always been drawn to you.* That's what I'm talking about. Again, it has to be real. But if you pay attention and look for the good, you can create an environment of acceptance.

And remember — unexpressed gratitude *feels like ingratitude.* Nothing makes a person's heart colder than feeling unappreciated.

YOUR PHYSICAL PRESENCE

We men are much "bigger" than we think we are. We take up more space. We're louder, we eat more, we're messier, smellier and make more bodily noises. Without realizing it, we can create an environment in our homes that reeks of selfishness. And where there is selfishness, there has to be service. Someone has to pick up the slack created by selfishness. That's often our wives, and it feels like rejection to them. They think, *He doesn't care about me; all he cares about is himself* (as you watch the ball game while she folds your underwear).

In an environment of acceptance . . . where a woman feels honored and cared for . . . would a man fart anytime he felt the urge? So get up, go the bathroom, shut the door and let it out where you're supposed to. Turn on the fan. Turn off the fan. You think it's funny. I assure you women don't. And yes, they do it too. But it's different for a man. Fair? No. Real? Yes. You say, *That's silly. I ain't doin' that.* Well, Mr. King of the Hill, just keep farting at will and you may end up free to fart wherever and whenever you want. 'Cause she'll be gone! Would you have farted around her when you were dating her? Of course not.

So what's changed?

Could be you take her for granted. You care less what she thinks. You've got your rights. It's your house, right? Haughtiness. Laziness. Selfishness — which requires service, which feels like rejection and lack of gratitude.

YOUR ROLE AT HOME

A lot of men who are leaders at work think they're automatically anointed "King Poobah" when they get home. It doesn't work that way.

You may have *authority* at work, but you're a *collaborator* at home. You can still lead, but if you're going to have a great marriage, you're going to have to learn to lead differently.

She's your partner. You're not her boss. She owns 50 percent of everything. (Get to divorce court and you may find out she owns more!) Treat her with the kind of respect you would an equal business partner. Don't give her instructions like you would a subordinate. Have conversations, make suggestions, listen to her opinions — and value them.

> **YOU MAY HAVE AUTHORITY AT WORK, BUT YOU'RE A COLLABORATOR AT HOME.**
> ————

Here's a new one for you. Ask *her* what *you* can do to help. Volunteer your services, just like you would with a business partner. You would never ask your business partner to pick up after you. You pick up after yourself at work. Why not do it at home? Dishes don't float from the sink to the dishwasher. Someone has to put them there. When they print "dishwasher safe," they're talking to us men. It's safe for us to put our own stuff in the dishwasher. Heck, you might even go crazy and put her dishes in there too. I've found my wife actually enjoys being served once in a while!

In an environment of acceptance, your wife would have freedom like you do. She wouldn't have to ask your permission for everything. And she would feel empowered, not second-guessed, if some of her decisions don't exactly match what you would have done.

THINK DIFFERENTLY

If you like the idea of creating an environment of acceptance, consider these three ideas:

1. *Lengthen your time horizon.* What's your long-term goal here? To be content. To have peace. To live in harmony. To have joy. To be successful. To love and be loved. All those things are very long-term; they don't happen overnight. Sacrifice your selfish, *I want it now,* for the longer view. Ask yourself, *Will creating an environment of acceptance, even if it's hard, move me toward my long-term goals?* I can tell you, trying to grab what you want, push your wife around, and "manage" her like an employee won't get you there.

2. *Don't sweat small stuff* – teach yourself to overlook things. Ignore more. If something bothers you, fix it yourself instead of blaming your wife and pressuring her to fix it. If you're smart enough to see it's wrong, you're smart enough to take care of it yourself. And keep your mouth shut.

3. *Find the positive.* You can teach yourself to find the positive. Start by saying something positive every time you say something negative. Work to get to a one-to-one ratio, positive for negative, and then grow from there. Let your wife hear you too. She's probably heard a lot of the bad . . . let her hear your voice say good things about her, about life, about anything.

THE CURSE OF CRITICISM

The enemy of acceptance is rejection — and to your wife, criticism feels like rejection, plain and simple. If you want to become a better husband, you will have to stop criticizing.

Here are some thoughts that may flash through your mind.

I'm just trying to help. I know she wants to do better.

She sure feels free to point things out to me. Why can't I do the same for her?

I don't mean to be critical. I'm just telling her what I see. She has a big blind spot!

If she'd just listen to me and deal with what I'm telling her, this would go away.   There wouldn't be any criticism!

Why do I have to be so careful about what I say? Am I going to spend the rest of my life walking on eggshells?

Half the time, I'm not even criticizing her when I say stuff. She's just hypersensitive. She takes everything personally!

Does any of that sound familiar?

Read on.

IT SUCKS TO BE CRITICIZED

Let me repeat myself. Nobody wants to be criticized. Nobody.

I used to think I wasn't affected by criticism. I welcomed it.

"I'm so hungry to learn, to be the best I can be, I embrace criticism. I want to find ways to improve, no matter who the criticism comes from or what it's about," — or so I thought.

I was full of it.

I figured out that criticism about things I've done is pretty easy to take. I *do* want to do better, to get better in relationships, to be wiser, and to make better decisions.

But when criticism hits on who *I am*, it's different. And almost all criticism hits on the "who" and not just the "what."

WHAT IS CRITICISM ANYWAY . . . REALLY?

Criticism requires a standard of comparison. The critic has to have a picture of what should or could be in his mind. When he sees "reality," he compares the actual to the standard and sees the differences. When he reveals these differences to the person who is out of line with what he thinks should or could be, that's criticism.

Sometimes there is an *objective* standard of comparison, like when your kid is about to board a ride at the amusement park. "You have to be this tall to ride," the sign says. No one gets his feelings hurt because the standard is clear; you stand beside the little bunny rabbit and if your head doesn't reach his hand, you don't ride.

But clear standards are rare. Most of what we compare people to is conjured up in our minds. *It's how my mama did it.* It's how someone looked on TV. It's what we saw portrayed in a movie. It's what we heard someone describe in a class we took or a book we read. And sometimes our standards are born of our own wishful thinking. We just make 'em up. *It should be this way because I'd like it this way.*

Criticism stems from judgment. When you're comparing something about your wife to someone else, or to a contrived standard you've come up with, you're judging. For judgment to happen, there has to be a judge, and you've set yourself up as that. In essence, you're saying, *I know what's good and what's not, and honey, you ain't good!* You may not mean to, but your self-righteousness and pumped-up view of yourself come screaming through.

That's how it felt in our marriage for the first 12 years. I had this vague, unwritten, unspoken idea of what she should be like, how she should look, what she should say and how she should respond in every situation. Only I knew what it was. And the only way she could find out was by ***not*** meeting my standard and getting criticized. After a while (a long while — she's a patient woman), she'd had enough. There was no environment of acceptance in our house . . . only rejection. She left.

THE WORD "YOU" IS A CLUE

As I said, a lot of our criticism is so ingrained . . . is such a habit . . . we aren't even aware we're doing it. Not long ago, I picked up on the word "you" . . . and how it seemed to always be there . . . just before the bomb went off.

> *"You know, if **you** would just plan our meals in advance, we wouldn't always be running out to the grocery store and eating so late."*
> *"That dress is pretty, but I'm not sure it suits you. I think **you** look better in something that fits a little looser."*
> *"If **you** would just try this, you might like it."*
> *"**You** always say stuff like that."*
> *"**You** never help me get the kids ready for bed."* You never give the bath
> *"Every time **you** talk to your sister, you come back crying and upset."*
> *"**You** used to enjoy watching the game with me."*

You are always on your phone.

Do you get it? Can you feel the rejection, the accusation, the criticism coming from the word "you"?

Let's think about what's really being said in each of these exchanges. I'll be your wife.

What you said: *You know, if **you** would just plan our meals in advance, we wouldn't always be running out to the grocery store and eating so late.*

What she felt: *He thinks I'm stupid, lazy, or both. He has no idea what I do.*

What you expected to hear: *Oh, you're right honey. I should be a better*

What I feel: time waster, bad MOM, lazy

planner. I'll work on it. I'll start keeping a better list of what we need and do more shopping in advance.

What you heard: *So why don't **you** try doing what I do for a few days? Let's see how dinner comes together when **you** do all the stuff I do! **You** have no concept of how hard it is to take care of this house and raise these kids. How dare **you** come in here and "coach" me on grocery shopping!*

And notice how many times the word "you" comes back your way. That feels like rejection to you. So it's on. You both feel criticized. You both feel rejected.

Here's another one . . .

What you said: *That dress is pretty, but I'm not sure it suits **you**. I think **you'd** look better in something that fits a little looser*

What she felt: *I'm not attractive.*

What you expected to hear: *Thanks, dear. I really want to look my best. I truly value your objective opinion. Now that I have a better idea of what you think will look good on me, why don't we leave the mall and go do something you want to do. I'll come back later and see what I can find.*

What you heard: ***You** have the fashion sense of a homeless man. **You've** got that potbelly, but all I hear about is my weight. I'd love to see **you** carry around a baby for nine months and then lose 35 pounds!*

One more . . .

What you said: *If **you** would just try this, **you** might like it.*

What she felt: *He doesn't love me enough to let me be me, to have my own likes and dislikes when they're different from his.*

What you expected to hear: **You're** *right.*

What you heard: *I don't want to try it. I'm 30 years old. I'm capable of deciding what I like and what I don't like!*

Imagine what she feels when she hears you say . . .

You *never help me get the kids ready for bed.*

Every time **you** *talk to your sister,* **you** *come back crying and upset.*

You *used to enjoy watching the game with me.*

Do you see how criticism sets off these emotions? Can you visualize how your wife feels when you say these idiotic little things? And how she'll retort out of her hurt, not out of her heart?

WHY SO SENSITIVE?

Little girls get a ton of their self-esteem from their dads — from guys like you and me.

That should be a clue!

Very few dads carefully build and protect their daughters' self-esteem when they're little. Some do a better job than others, but a tiny percentage of women come out of adolescence feeling lovely and lovable.

They grow up . . . and we come along and sweep them off their feet. We tell them how lovely they are. We woo them, romance them and chase after them like a dog chasing a school bus. They feel lovely. Healthy. Fulfilled by the passion of a young man's pursuit. They marry us and within no time, the wooing stops, the romance ends and they're questioning the very essence of their self-esteem. *If he doesn't pursue me anymore and all he sees are my faults,* *then I must **not** be lovely.* And from that anxiety, from not feeling good about herself, comes defensiveness. She'll protect herself by criticizing you back. And it's on!

And here's the surprise part . . .

She really **wants** to please you.

Or at least she wanted to. If you're like me, you make it impossible by constantly "moving the cheese". . . making it so she never really knows what you want from her. Trying to please me was like trying to stand in the corner of a round room. It was impossible.

IT NEVER WORKS, SO WHY . . .

Think back to one time — just one — when you criticized your wife and it came out well. Tell me about one time when you criticized her and she came back with . . .

> *Oh, you're right honey. I should be a better planner. I'll work on it. I'll start keeping a better list of what we need and do more shopping in advance.*

Or . . .

> *Thank you for reminding me that what I'm about to eat will make me gain weight. I didn't know that. I'm going to throw it out, go on a diet and start exercising. Where would I be without you to show me the way?*

Silly, huh?

Look: Criticism never works.

Never.

So stop giving it!

Be aware of your thoughts and catch the critical ones before they come out of your mouth. Wrestle them to the ground. Walk them back from your lips and erase them from your mind.

Leave your wife alone.

Choose to accept her as she is and never criticize her — never criticize what she does — ever again.

. . . AND HER MOTHER TOO!

One other point. If you and your wife are at odds, there's a very high probability that you and your mother-in-law are not big fans of each other. You've heard your wife say not-so-nice things about her mom and you've joined in.

You've stepped in the trap!

Newsflash! Your wife can say anything she wants about her mother. *But you can't.* When you say the exact same thing your wife says — word for word — it sounds different to her. Meaner. More venomous. Even if she agrees with everything you say, she'll turn on you. Face it. It's a fact of life.

NEWSFLASH! YOUR WIFE CAN SAY ANYTHING SHE WANTS ABOUT HER MOTHER. BUT YOU CAN'T.

You have to learn to *stay quiet* when she's blasting her mom. *Never* join in. No matter what she says or does, keep your mouth shut. She may be the meanest witch in the West, but she's not *your* mother. And there's a bond between a daughter and her mom that's impossible for a man to understand. Stay mum about mom.

OFFENSE AND DEFENSE:
ACCEPTANCE AND THE ABSENCE OF CRITICISM

In football, they say offense wins games but defense wins championships. Think about creating acceptance as playing offense . . . scoring points. Defense is dropping the criticism. I say start there.

If your marriage is in a good place, you're probably already dishing out a lot of affirmation. Paying compliments. Expressing gratitude. Keep that going, but also pay attention to criticism you may be leaking out. Squash it. Catch yourself and learn to stifle the critic inside.

If your marriage is less-than-great, but not in trouble, your wife may be so used to your criticism it hardly seems to affect her. She's tuned it out or become so calloused, it doesn't hurt anymore. But if you will be *proactive* to create a positive acceptance vibe, your wife will feel it. And if you'll dial down the comments and dial up the (genuine) compliments . . . words of affirmation and gratitude . . . your wife will be drawn to you and things may move in a direction and at a pace you never imagined.

If you're in trouble at home, cut the criticism and train yourself to accept your wife just as she is. You'll be shocked at how quickly things can turn around. Women are sensitive . . . very sensitive. They feel things deeply. When we turn our cuts into compliments, get behind them as people and give them the affirmation of being accepted, we start a warm fire in the heart. A fire with warmth we will enjoy for the rest of our lives.

RADICAL HUSBANDS don't criticize their wives. They create environments of acceptance instead.

STEP
SIX

LEARN TO
LISTEN

*A woman who feels she has no "voice" is a
woman whose husband does not connect to
her feelings.*

I remember it like it was yesterday.

It was years past our "crisis." I thought I had figured it out. Things were going well.

We were having a conversation about something, whether to buy something, replace something… I can't remember what. It wasn't a heated discussion. As a matter of fact, whatever we were talking about wasn't even all that important. As was *always* the case with us, she saw it one way and I saw it another.

All of a sudden, Miriam just blew up: "You never *really* listen to me. I have no 'voice' on anything. You just do what you're going to do. I don't even know why you bother talking to me about these things!"

Her words pierced my soul: "I have no voice!"

What Radical Husbands Do • **69**

That hurt.

And I was the one who brought it up. I was the one who asked for her opinion. I was the one seeking her input. What did I miss here?

I don't want to be the kind of husband who walks all over his wife. I had to figure this out.

EVERYONE NEEDS A VOICE

Last year, some friends of ours got into trouble. The wife reached out to Miriam. Guess what she said?

"I don't feel like I have a voice!"

They had decided to get a new car—for her. It was going to be the everyday "family wagon" for her and their two boys. She wanted a minivan, but that didn't fit with her husband's picture of what they should have. "*We need a big, safe SUV,*" he barked. And he went out and bought one. The car became an icon, a symbol of the way he treated her, how he ignored her "voice." After kicking this "voice" question around for a while, my friend John came up with the answer. He said, "Show me a woman with no "voice," and I'll show you a woman whose husband has failed to acknowledge his wife's ***feelings***."

Bingo!

It brought back the conversation with Miriam. The *facts* about the decision didn't set her off. I had failed to acknowledge her *feelings*.

Chances are your wife feels this way sometimes — maybe a lot of the time, especially if things aren't going well. Even if you try to listen and acknowledge her feelings, you don't know how.

So I'm going to teach you some basic listening skills. They build on each other.

The first one is really basic. The second one is harder. And the third one, if you catch on to it, will help you begin to connect with your wife's feelings. That's when you'll start to make real progress in your relationship.

BABY LISTENING STEP 1 — ATTENDING

Attending is the first level of listening. It simply involves positioning yourself to pay attention when your wife speaks and to let her know you're listening.

Here are the elements to manage:

1. *Where you are and what's going on.* Turn off the television, the radio, the stereo, the Internet — anything that will distract you or her. Don't be weird about it, but communicate that you care by giving her your undivided attention.

2. *How you sit.* Face her, if at all possible. Keep your hands still. Don't fidget, tap your fingers, wring your hands or twist your wedding ring (which, by the way, behavioral scientists say signals that you're in a situation you want out of).

   Don't fiddle with your pen, your watch or your smart phone. Don't fiddle with anything. Sit straight; don't slouch. By your posture, you communicate that you're tuned in and paying attention. Maintain this posture throughout the conversation. You're telling her, *What you're saying is important enough for me to sit up and take notice.* Don't be unnatural about it, but *start paying attention to how you're paying attention* — or not.

3. *Your eyes.* She will decide if you're listening by your eyes. She can't tell if your ears are tuned in, but your eyes will tell the story. Establish and maintain appropriate eye contact. What's "appropriate"? Look into her eyes, but don't stare. Most people naturally glance away every few seconds when they're in a conversation. "Appropriate" means staying connected, looking away only for a split second to relieve the tension, both yours and

hers. That feels normal and natural. (Just don't have ESPN on the tube so when you look away, you're checking the score!)

That's it. That's the first step in active listening. Simply managing the environment so there aren't distractions; sitting so your posture says you're not bored, nervous or dying to get outta there; and keeping a posture so you can make comfortable, consistent eye contact. Again, look into her eyes when she's speaking. Let her know with your eyes, a nod of your head, a little smile that you care and you're really listening.

You can do this if you try. This takes no special skill, just a desire to say, *Hey, you're important enough to me that I want to really hear what you have to say.* If this sounds silly and you're thinking, Hey, I'm not doing this, you have a pride problem. Humble yourself. Be teachable. Try some new stuff. You need to be a better listener, no matter what. You can't lose by learning these skills.

Starting the next time you're around her, I want you to practice this. Practice "attending" to her. Practice it with others too. Form the habit of looking at the person you're supposed to be listening to, maintaining appropriate eye contact and showing them you're listening by managing your body.

BABY LISTENING STEP 2 – CONTENT RESPONDING

Now that you're "tuned in," looking into her eyes and paying attention, start listening for content — the what of what she's saying. Then respond by letting her know that you really heard what she said.

Here's a harsh fact. People don't listen to each other. As soon as you think you know what she's saying, you tune out. You'll finish her sentence for her, or you'll drift off and start subconsciously planning what you're going to say in response. Either way, you've stopped listening and people know it, especially our wives.

Now, you're going to listen to what she says and you're going to say it back to her. You'll feel like a parrot at first, but that's okay.

When she says something like, *My mother isn't doing very well. She's planning to go back to the doctor on Tuesday*, you're going to say, *You said your mother isn't doing very well, and she's planning to go back to the doctor on Tuesday?*

I know it sounds stupid. Cheesy. Repetitive.

But until you try it, you won't recognize how bad a listener you've become.

The first thing that'll hit you is how you'll *interpret* what she says and twist it into something she didn't say or mean.

You'll come up with, *You said your mom is sick and she's going to the doctor.*

That's not what your wife said. She said, *She's not doing very well*, not that she's sick. And the fact that *she's going back to the doctor on Tuesday* may be the reason your wife is telling you this. She may be thinking of going to the doctor with her. She may be tacitly looking for your permission and you missed the whole point by only partially hearing what she said.

Picky?

Yes.

Realistic?

Yes.

Try it with a friend or someone from work. Sit down face-to-face. Have the other person say a paragraph to you. Then repeat it. *You said . . .* and say back **exactly** what he said to you. It's tough to do. Really tough.

Why is it so hard?

For one reason, we're always in a hurry. We just want the minimum, the essence, the least amount of info so we can decide what to do next. We don't *really* care what they're saying. We just want to get what we need and get going.

Sometimes it's because of low self-esteem. We spend our emotional energy trying to take care of ourselves and have little left for others. Subconsciously, we're wondering what they're thinking *about us*. So much so, we have no emotional capacity for them. If this is you, the answer to this one is in the last chapter. But don't read ahead. Stick with me here.

Practice "content responding." Listen to your wife, your kids and your workmates, and see if you can say back to them what they say to you. If they catch on to what you're doing and call you out, tell them the truth. *I'm working on my listening skills. I'm learning to be a better listener.* They'll be impressed, whether they admit it or not.

BABY LISTENING STEP 3 — THE "FEELING" RESPONSE

Here's where you can start to connect with your wife's feelings and make real progress. This is the hardest one, but the one most often rewarded when it's learned.

Listen to what your wife is saying (the content), but also pay attention to her emotions.

What word describes the emotion she is feeling right now?

Let's go back to the example we used before:

> *My mother isn't doing very well. She's planning to go back to the doctor on Tuesday.*

Watching her eyes, listening to the tone of her voice, watching her facial expressions, you see concern or worry or abject fear. You land on "concern" as the word that best describes her feelings.

You're concerned about your mom, aren't you? you say.

Yes! she says, as she looks at you and thinks, Who stole my husband and replaced him with this guy who's really listening to me?

Be ready, because listening to her feelings and using the right "feeling word" will open her up. Because she feels that you care, she'll tell you more about what she's thinking, how she's feeling or maybe even what she's ultimately afraid of.

This is what you're after. This is what you want. You want her to open up, to trust you with her feelings. She wants to be understood, and connecting with how she's feeling in the moment gives her that.

One key: The emotion you're trying to read is her emotion *right now.* It's not how she felt when she was on the phone with her mom. It's the emotion she's feeling and showing while she's talking to you. That's what you're listening for.

Let's suppose you get it wrong. You say, *You're worried about your mom.* That's not what she's feeling, so she might say, *No, I'm not really worried, at least not yet. I'm just a little concerned.* She might go on to talk about her mother's previous health issues, or how her mother is "just like grandma" or whatever. Even though she corrected you, she also revealed the emotion she's actually feeling. And because you were willing to take a risk and guess at her feelings, you were rewarded. She feels cared for — you listened — she feels loved.

Feeling responses are guesses. We can't really *know* how another person feels at a moment in time. But when we pay attention, listen to *the content* of what she's saying, read the emotion in her voice, her face and her eyes, and then

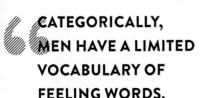

CATEGORICALLY, MEN HAVE A LIMITED VOCABULARY OF FEELING WORDS.

make a guess with a feeling word, we lean toward her emotionally. If we read her emotion accurately, we'll see her eyes light up. She can't help it. We all "light up" when someone understands how we feel.

Categorically, men have a limited vocabulary of feeling words. One mom said if she doesn't do anything else for her sons, she's going to teach them a lot of feeling words so they'll be able to express their feelings *and* be able to listen well to the feelings of others when they grow up.

There are numerous lists of feeling words out there. Read through these and see how many you use everyday in talking with your wife.

HAPPY

festive	glad	sparkling
contented	pleased	merry
relaxed	grateful	generous
calm	cheerful	hilarious
complacent	excited	exhilarated
satisfied	cheery	jolly
serene	lighthearted	playful
comfortable	buoyant	elated
peaceful	carefree	jubilant
joyous	surprised	thrilled
ecstatic	optimistic	restful
enthusiastic	spirited	silly
inspired	vivacious	giddy

ANGRY

contemptuous	sullen	boiling
resentful	indignant	fuming
irritated	irate	stubborn
enraged	wrathful	belligerent
furious	cross	confused
annoyed	sulky	awkward
inflamed	bitter	bewildered
provoked	frustrated	
offended	grumpy	

AFRAID

fearful	alarmed	suspicious
frightened	cautious	hesitant
timid	shocked	awed
wishy-washy	horrified	dismayed
shaky	insecure	scared
apprehensive	impatient	cowardly
fidgety	nervous	threatened
terrified	dependent	appalled
panicky	anxious	petrified
tragic	pressured	gutless
hysterical	worried	edgy

SAD

Sorrowful	flat	concerned
unhappy	blah	sympathetic
depressed	dull	compassionate
melancholy	in the dumps	choked up
gloomy	sullen	embarrassed
somber	moody	shameful
dismal	sulky	ashamed
heavy-hearted	out	useless
quiet	low	worthless
mournful	discontented	ill at ease
dreadful	discouraged	weepy
dreary	disappointed	vacant

One more thing to note.

Feeling words range from generic to specific. The more specifically the word matches what a person is feeling at a moment in time, the more that person will feel he or she was listened to (and cared about). The more generic the word, the weaker the impact.

When you start trying this, you'll find yourself saying things like, *You feel concerned,* or *You feel interested.* Yeah, but so what? If you're awake, you're concerned. If you're in a conversation at all, you're interested. Those are safe words, but not specific enough to be emotive.

Not too long ago, I was sitting down to lunch with a friend. I could see tension all over his face. As soon as we exchanged small talk and the waitress brought our menus, I said, "John, you seem pensive." It was like I set off a fireworks display. He started telling me all the issues he was dealing with, problems with his kids, stressors at work — the works. It showed me once again the power of picking the right feeling word to "open someone up."

FIXING IT

What I'm about to tell you is vitally important. It's huge. Critical.

Listen to your wife, but don't try to fix things for her!

Ninety-nine percent of the time, she just wants you to know how she feels. She **does not** want your opinion, your assessment of the situation, your prescription for the cure or your advice about what she should say or do. If she wants your advice, she'll ask for it. My friend Ted sometimes asks his wife, "Do you want me to fix it or feel it?" She almost always answer "Just feel it." There's a smart boy.

We can score huge points just by listening to our wives and then accidentally flush those points down the commode by opening our big mouths. Saying things like, "Here's what you should do," or "If she were my sister, I'd . . .". You can instantly kill all the good you did by listening.

If you just can't help yourself, if you just have to say something, try this:

Is there anything I can do to help you with this?

What you're likely to hear is, *No, I'm okay. I just wanted to talk it through with you.*

Miriam calls it "processing." She processes relationships and situations as she talks to me about them. She's not asking for my advice. She's just thinking it through as she's telling me. I've learned that simply listening empathetically, giving her occasional content and feeling responses, is all I need to do. At the end of the day, she feels listened to.

And you rarely go wrong with a big long hug.

That's called loving your wife.

Listening is loving. RADICAL HUSBANDS listen.

GIVE UP
SEX

*Recognize that your drive for sex
may be killing your marriage. Give it up.
If sex happens, it has to be mutual.*

For the first 12 years of our marriage, I wanted sex all the time. Every day. I pushed, pressured, manipulated — whatever it took. I was crazy. It didn't matter what time of the month, what else was going on in life or where we were, I wanted sex. Period.

I'm not sure I even knew what intimacy was. But I sure knew what sex was.

Then suddenly, she was gone. She left. Having sex wasn't an option.

When she came back, it was a new game . . . a new day.

It was back to courting. I had to love her, woo her, and win her heart if I was to have sex. By then, we were so far apart emotionally, it wasn't going to happen "because I said so." It wasn't going to happen because I wanted it. If it happened, it was because she felt close to me and felt enough love for me that she also wanted sex, both to please me and herself.

SEX AND INTIMACY

You don't need a definition of sex. But you may need one for intimacy.

The dictionary says intimacy is "emotional warmth and closeness."

You know when you're "in the zone" of warmth and closeness. You know when you're on the same page. The distractions dissipate, the conversation flows, there is absolutely no criticism, no friction in the conversation. There's no, *Can we have sex or not?* It just happens.

For women, the best kind of sex . . . the only *desirable* kind of sex . . . is from the overflow of intimacy. It's when she loves you so much in the moment, *she wants* to go to bed with you. It may be that she wants to give you what you want and need. It may be that she wants to love and be loved physically and sensually for herself. Or it may be both. Regardless, great sex flows from intimacy.

 FOR WOMEN, THE BEST KIND OF SEX . . . THE ONLY DESIRABLE KIND OF SEX . . . IS FROM THE OVERFLOW OF INTIMACY.

Men think it doesn't matter, but it does. For years, I thought, "If we can just have sex and 'get the pressure off,' then I'll relax and be intimate."

I was wrong.

Maybe I'm just turning into a "girly man," but I've found that I enjoy sex much more when it starts with intimacy. I've even found myself passing up the opportunity because *I didn't feel close to Miriam!* (Maybe something is wrong with me!)

5 FEET FOR 5 MINUTES

Lovemaking starts when you walk in the door. If you've been at work and she's been home, or if she gets home from work before you, how you "re-engage" is huge.

For years, I've been teaching this simple little practice called "5 for 5." It's made a huge difference for a ton of guys. Here's how it goes . . .

LOVEMAKING STARTS WHEN YOU WALK IN THE DOOR.

When you walk in the door, go directly to within five feet of your wife. Don't look at the paper; don't play with the dog; don't shuffle through the mail. Go directly to her. Then stay there for the first five minutes you're home. Make eye contact. You might give her a hug or maybe a kiss, depending on the dynamics of your relationship, but that's not the point. What matters is that you "vote" your *first minutes* of coming home to the person who is *first in your life*. You camp out in her personal space. You can give nonsexual touches. Touch her shoulder. Squeeze her hand . . . that kind of thing. But your mission is to listen to her. "Attend" to her. Ask her about her day, but this time, really listen and care about what she tells you. Stay in her frame of reference. Save "your stuff" for later — dinner — whenever. This time is *about her and for her*.

What about the kids? you ask.

This is your chance to teach them patience and, at the same time, to visibly model how a loving husband treats his wife. Some guys I know use something called "couch time" as a way to manage the kids while they do "5 for 5." Couch time says, *Go to the couch and wait. You can read, play games, do whatever you want to do while staying on the couch, but until I tell you, you can't interrupt Mom and me, and you can't leave the couch.*

My friend Dayne decided to give "5 for 5" a try. His kids struggled with giving him up when he first came home. They were so used to roughhousing and getting "first dibs" on Dad. But Dayne insisted on "couch time" and he prevailed — sort of.

One day as he and Anne were catching up in their "5-for-5" time, Dayne noticed his son slip quietly into the kitchen. His son started emptying the dishwasher, something his mom and dad didn't know he even knew how to do.

What are you doing, Jackson? his dad asked.

I'm helping out so you and Mommy can keep talking!

Kids love to see their parents loving each other. It makes them feel secure. Conversely, when they see their parents argue, they're fearful and often wonder if their home is safe. They can even think it's their fault.

"5 feet for 5 minutes" isn't magic. But it's a practice that can strengthen your relationship and it's an on-ramp to intimacy. When you and your wife get on the same page when you first reunite after work, there's a better chance that good things will happen later in the evening.

EXCLUSIVITY

I'm betting that there's some stuff going on with you sexually. Here's why I'm probably right.

- Between 50 and 60 percent of men have an affair sometime before age 60. The percentage of women is between 40 and 50%.
- 25 percent of American men have visited a porn sight in the last 30 days.
- Of the people who divorce, almost 50 percent cite infidelity as the reason.

Kinsey Institute statistics

Sex is like epoxy. There are two ingredients required for it to work, and you only control one. Your wife controls the other. You have two choices: you can find another source, or you can decide that you're going to "lock in" to your wife as the source. That means "locking out" everyone else. Exclusivity. No matter how long it takes or what it costs you.

Here's something you can try. It worked for me.

Think back to the best sex you ever had with your wife. You can remember it vividly. There was something visual about it; that's why you remember it so well. Get that picture in your head. Call up that "film sequence" in minute detail. Try to remember everything about it: where you were, the smells, the temperature, what she was wearing (or not wearing), her skin, what she did, how it felt, everything you saw — everything. Now go over it again. And again. And again.

Every time you think about sex, replay that tape. Flash back to your wife, your own beautiful wife, someone who is real, who is accessible, who might actually still love you. Relive that experience.

Make the decision . . . right now . . . that this is the only "tape" you're going to play. Decide that whenever you think about sex, you're going to replay that tape; you're going to call up the images of her and not someone else. From this moment forward, lust after your own wife, no one else.

I'M NO PSYCHOLOGIST, BUT . . .

Here's what I've figured out. There are unanswered questions down deep inside of me.

- Do I measure up?
- Do I have what it takes?
- I don't have to be the best, but am I good enough?

When your wife has sex with you and she lets go, gets into it, truly enjoys it, that little voice down deep inside says, *Yeah, you're good. You have what it takes. You're good enough!* You get the affirmation you want and need as a man. She could be totally faking it, but your subconscious noggin says, *I'm okay.*

FROM THIS MOMENT FORWARD, LUST AFTER YOUR OWN WIFE, NO ONE ELSE.

The trick is to recognize what's happening and put it in perspective. Is *Do I measure up as a man?* really answered by how hard she breathes when you make love to her? Is your manhood truly validated by her orgasm? Or could it be that sex is a surrogate for true validation? True affirmation?

What if character turns out to be more affirming and more validating than sexual performance?

Or better, what if it's both? What if developing strong character (doing the right thing even when no one is looking) actually *leads* to sexual fulfillment? What if being the right kind of man inside *attracts your wife* and draws her to you sexually?

Here's one final challenge, and it has to do with controlling your vessel. Can you decide to think with your brain and not with your "Johnson"? Is the act of sex so important to you that you'd risk everything you have, everything you could possibly have, just to have those few minutes of pleasure? Why is it *that* important? Can't you wait, just for a while, and work on the nonsexual parts of your marriage?

If you were sent off to war for a year, wouldn't you wait?

You'd *have* to.

So choose to give up sex for now.

Instead of trying to make it happen, RADICAL HUSBANDS create intimacy, choose exclusivity and let sex come to them.

LEARN TO LOSE

*Men have this instinctive need to win, to be right
(or at least not be wrong). We destroy our wives with our
thoughtless push to prevail.*

By now, you're probably thinking, "This book was written by a woman posing as a man. The ideas are so 'one-sided,' so anti-husband and so pro-wife. Why don't you come clean, Mr. Campbell, and confess your secret female identity?"

Not so, but thanks for playing.

I'm as male as anyone can be. And that "maleness" is what took my marriage to the brink.

A big part of being male is winning . . . and not knowing how to lose. Most of us are competitive, whether we want to admit it or not. Look at the games we play. If we're pretty good (translated: can compete), we'll play that game. If we're not, we won't. People who are not good enough to be competitive at golf with their friends give up the game. Same with tennis, soccer, ultimate Frisbee or ping pong. Even board games and card games.

How many times have you heard someone say, *I always win at poker, so I gave it up?*

Be honest: How hard is it to lose, to just give up, to fly the white flag and surrender?

Now if you asked me, *Do you think you always have to win?* I'd say, *No, absolutely not. Nobody wins all the time.* But emotionally, losing is hard to swallow. Period.

So what are we talking about here? What competition am I learning to lose?

I'm talking about conflict.

Any conflict.

YOU'VE STEPPED ON IT

It begins the moment you realize you just crossed over the line. You've struck a nerve, or she's struck one in you. It goes downhill from there.

The relationally gifted among us recognize those land mines and stop before stepping on them. There are men who keep quiet. I'm sure of it. They can stop themselves on a dime, holding back that one line that's going to set her off. They can hold themselves back and not let what she says set them off. It's like they have a sixth sense. They smell the conflicts that wait on the other side of their responses, and they stop right there. God bless them. I wish I were one of them.

I'm like many of you. I have a hard time holding my tongue when she says something that's wrong. I try to explain the "truth" to her and it's on. And she doesn't think I have feelings. She can say anything in the world about me and never think how it sounded or how it made me feel.

Now here's the reality. She isn't going to change her mind. And you aren't going to change yours. How many times have you stepped into the ring, gone a few rounds and had her say, *Whoa! You're right. I totally missed it. You're right and I'm wrong. Will you please forgive me?* Even if the facts are researched and what you thought to be true is true, you still lost. You made her feel bad. And now you feel bad, even after you have the facts. You lost — *even though you won.*

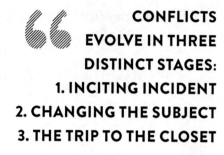

CONFLICTS EVOLVE IN THREE DISTINCT STAGES: 1. INCITING INCIDENT 2. CHANGING THE SUBJECT 3. THE TRIP TO THE CLOSET

Conflicts evolve in three distinct stages.

First, there's the *inciting incident.* This is usually something I say, a piece of unsolicited advice, a phrase added to an innocent sentence that includes a small amount of correction of a recollection of how something happened that is different from how she remembers it. These are inciting incidents of the spoken variety. And most arguments stem from things that are spoken.

The momentum then builds as the retorts go back and forth, each with a little more emotion, a little more venom and getting a little more off the original subject, which leads to the second phase of the argument: *changing the subject.*

A comment like, *Your fried chicken is great, but your mom makes the best fried chicken ever. I think it's the Crisco she fries it in. I don't know how she does it, but it's special.*

Then the retort: *So my chicken isn't so hot, huh? Well, thank you very much. I cook it just like my mom does. My mom never uses Crisco. You never cook with my mom. . . . You have no idea what she cooks with. You never take the time to get to know my mom!*

The subject is no longer the fried chicken. It's, *You don't love my mother.* A totally different subject. How did that happen?

Which leads to the next phase of the argument, which I call *the trip to the closet.*

> *Do you remember that time on vacation when Mom wanted to sit and talk about old times? You just walked away and went outside. I saw the tears well up in her eyes. I couldn't believe you were so insensitive.*

In this phase, she's gone to the closet (where memories from the past are stored) and pulled out a perfect example of when you passed up the opportunity to spend time with her mother. (Notice how far we are from the fried chicken.)

You are the poor underdog male who has insufficient horsepower to even stay in this race — much less win.

And before you think I'm blaming or belittling the female element, I know we men do the same thing. In the heat of battle, we'll pull out old boyfriends, twenty-year-ago screw-ups, and *Remember when you* (fill in the blank).

The true hurt comes when it gets personal. You say things like, *You're just like your mother,* or she says, *You're not the man I thought you were.* These are the words that can't be taken back. They break emotional bones. They leave marks and scars.

If any of these conversations sounds familiar, you've got some forgiveness to ask for. It'll pay you to replay the tapes of the last several conflicts you had with your wife. Take pen and paper in hand and write down what you said — word for word. You'll be tempted to lie to yourself to make it sound better, but don't. Be accurate. Then focus on just two of the nasty things you've said, and get ready to confess that you shouldn't have said them. Tell her you're sorry, and ask her to forgive you. If you don't get a response, just say, *I understand. Hopefully, you'll be able to forgive me someday. I'm going to hold on to that hope, and I'm going to show you I'm sincerely sorry by not using hurtful words like that again.* But then you gotta live it.

Assuming you "step on it" often, either by putting her on the defensive or defending yourself, what do you do? How can you learn to lose?

DROP THE ROPE

"take off the gloves"

The most helpful idea I've heard is "drop the rope." A friend of mine authored this concept and it's helped a lot of people.

Imagine a tug-of-war. You're holding one end of the rope, and she's holding the other. As soon as you feel her tug, you drop the rope. You don't resist. The facts are still the same, but the pressure never materializes. You simply refuse to tug back. You opt out of an emotional response.

Now don't let this turn into the silent treatment. That's not good.

And you can't be dishonest or disingenuous. You don't have to lie or compromise your view of the truth. You simply drop the rope at the first tug and disarm the live, emotional grenade.

The people who win at tug-of-war go a step further. They pay attention to the other side and anticipate when the big tug is coming. If you'll learn to pay attention to your wife, you will see stuff coming and be ready to drop the rope before it's tugged. If you work at it, you can teach yourself not to tug the rope. (They used to say, "Pull her chain," but that doesn't sound good.)

Understand: I'm not a psychologist. I'm a business guy who's recovering from a serious case of defensiveness. Couple that with a critical spirit, and you've got a man who's very hard to be married to. So I don't share this (or any) idea out of strength. It's out of weakness.

Remember, in "Don't sweat the small stuff," it's **all** small stuff. Counselors are constantly amazed at the petty things that start huge fights — fights that lead to contempt and, ultimately, divorce.

As you try to win and keep your wife's heart, you're dealing with heightened sensitivities. If she's kind of "done with you," she's going to sense every sliver of criticism, sarcasm and negativity on your part. If you have any chance of making this marriage work, you've got to learn to lose.

Let things she says slide right on by. Don't get drawn into conflicts where the worst of both of you comes out. You're trying to show her a better side of you. If you pick the battle back up, you'll give up any ground you've gained.

RADICAL HUSBANDS drop the rope. RADICAL HUSBANDS learn to lose.

SET HER FREE

*If you free the bird and it comes back,
it's yours. If you set it free and it doesn't,
it wasn't yours to begin with.*

ou don't *have* a wife like you *have* a car. She's not a possession. She's a person.

In America, wives are volunteers. They choose to get married. They choose to stay married. They are free.

So setting her free sounds unnecessary, but it's not.

If we're honest, we'll admit that most of us want to control our wives to some degree. We want sex when we want it. We want them to do what we want them to do when we want them to do it. Since we're a little insecure of their love, we'd rather not give them opportunities to see what they're missing. We like to be in control.

A guy I know was so down on his wife, he was trying to "freeze her out," to

> **IF WE'RE HONEST, WE'LL ADMIT THAT MOST OF US WANT TO CONTROL OUR WIVES TO SOME DEGREE.**
> _____

make her feel so uncomfortable and unloved, she would leave and give him the upper hand in the divorce settlement. He said she wouldn't engage, wouldn't talk, wouldn't go places or do things with him. In a fit of rage one night, he took the battery out of her car. It showed his real issue. He said he wanted emotional engagement, but what he really wanted was control.

Don't get me wrong. I'm not heading toward some "open marriage" baloney. I'm just saying a lot of men like to be in control of women. And women resent it and run from it. They want the same thing we want — what all people want — autonomy. They want to make decisions, be trusted, feel empowered and prove their competence. And we want that for them . . . to a degree . . . as long as it doesn't threaten our little worlds or egos.

After one of our many relocations, Miriam hit the wall. Two small kids, a new city. Surrounded by strangers, husband traveling constantly. She was depressed.

CAUGHT UNAWARE

Men are terribly myopic. We only see things through our own eyes. When we move our families, it's usually for better jobs. We get excited. Fired up. We're going to make more money, gain status and receive accolades. We meet new people right away. We're thrust into new situations where we have to crank it up to make good first impressions and prove we were the right pick for the job. We have effortless access to new friends through our work. We go at it hard and drag ourselves home dead tired.

What we find at home are lonely families. Wives who have moved in support of their husbands have been ripped away from their homes, families and network of friends. Wives who work outside the home are faced with finding a new job, and that's a huge stressor. The kids don't know anyone and don't have playmates. The hard work of making a new house a home falls on wives — usually with limited budgets and often with little support from us. Before we know it, we're happily engaged in the new place and they're . . . well, they can be *depressed*.

In a particularly frank conversation, Miriam told me how trapped she felt when we moved, that she didn't feel like she could breathe. She didn't know her way around; she hadn't made any friends yet. She was dependent on me for everything. And I was gone, traveling four nights a week for my new job.

We figured something out. If she had a little bit of money that was hers — guilt-free money — it would help. She would feel a little bit of freedom. I could have gotten all squirrelly, suspicious or even paranoid. But I sensed she just needed some freedom, and I was right. We opened a bank account just for her. Not much money, but it was freedom.

Later, she signed up for a pottery course. It meant getting a sitter, driving around in the big new city and coming home late. But that too translated "freedom" to her.

SOMETIMES IT'S IMPORTANT TO STATE THE OBVIOUS.

FREE BIRD

When Miriam left me . . . when she'd had enough . . . she got in the car and drove away. I might have thought I had some degree of control. But I didn't. If I'd said no and hidden the keys, she'd have found a way to leave. One way or another, someone who wants out will eventually find a way out.

Guys, I think it's smart to lean into this, not to pull away from it. Acknowledge the obvious: *Hey, I want you to know I recognize that you're free. I accept the fact you don't have to do what I say or what I want you to do.* Sometimes it's important to state the obvious.

Start thinking about how you can give her more freedom. Resist the temptation to have some big powwow where you're going to sob and tell her how you love her so much you're setting her free. Malarkey.

Instead, *think*.

Think about what she really enjoys that she's not able to do right now. If she needs a babysitter for the kids, then take the initiative and find one for her . . . or do it yourself. Whether she works inside or outside the home, giving her free time is going to be hard. Taking care of your kids, all by yourself, might just be really good for you . . . and for them. You can do it. Talk about sending a strong message of genuine love!

If it's money holding her back, find a way to fund her project or hobby. Give up a few golf games; cancel ESPN (talk about sacrificial love!); do whatever it takes to find the money so she can pursue something that'll make her feel free.

If she works at home and spends most of her time raising kids, she may not be able to come up with anything at first. But if she's given some "guilt-free time" and a little money, she'll find something to explore and engage with. Cooking classes, college or graduate-degree courses, painting, pottery or business classes. You've probably heard her mention something like this. Maybe she wants to volunteer or get a part-time job, to have some time away from the kids or maybe to make a little money of her own. Get behind that idea if you can. Support her; don't discourage her. Even if you think her "thing" is a mistake, keep your mouth shut and let her make it. Let her go and learn for herself. If she were to leave you, she wouldn't even ask for your input. Isn't it better to be a supporter than an obstacle, especially since she ultimately has the freedom to do what she wants anyway? You want her to see you on her side, supporting her desire to "have a life."

The "win" here is for you to change your attitude and approach so she'll be drawn to you. It's to instill in you the confidence that you can "let go" and empower her to do things she wants to do. And she'll still come back to you.

Can you muster up the courage to be a RADICAL HUSBAND and set her free?

STEP
TEN

THINK
LONG-TERM

---

*It's not just about what comes next, but what your life will look like
down the road when your kids are married, you're a grandfather,
you're not as sexually active or attractive, you're old and sick.*

ight now is ***not*** all there is.

"Live for today, for tomorrow never comes," is a lie.

Tomorrow *will* come. You *will* get older. Your wife *will* change. You *will* qualify
for Social Security, unless the grim reaper snags you early.

Impatience is what gets a marriage in trouble. You want what you want, and
you want it now. Same with your wife. Little by little, one of you loses hope
that things will change, and the result is a mess of a marriage that hangs by a
thread.

I want to challenge you to take a minute and think long-term. Really *think*.

What Radical Husbands Do • 99

RIGHT NOW IS NOT ALL THERE IS.

THE DEATH OF DELAYED GRATIFICATION

As a culture, we're killing the idea of suffering now for the good stuff later. The divorce rate among young couples has dropped below 26 percent. Why? Because they're living together first. Have sex, live together, *then* make commitment and get married.

We want the new car and the newest, coolest stuff, but we don't want to save for them. We want them now. The answer? Car loans, credit card payments and oppressive debt.

We want happiness and we want it now. The idea of waiting for your mate to mature seems ridiculous. *What if she doesn't? What if she stays the spoiled "daddy's girl" until she dies? What if she never changes her attitude about sex? Are you ready to wait around till the kids leave home so maybe she'll become your lover again?*

And she's probably got the same questions about you. Will he ever grow up? Will his relentless pursuit of getting in my pants ever subside? Will he ever care as much about me as he does about his job? Will I ever get as much attention as the TV? Or the ball game? Will there ever be a time when he'll hang out with me as much as he plays golf? Will he ever learn to listen to me? Value what I value? Truly be my friend?

The answer is yes. It can happen. All of this is possible.

But it won't be overnight. It will take time, effort and a lot of patience. It's a long-term deal.

THE ESSENCE OF CHOICE

When I first heard what I'm about to tell you, I threw up all over it. But I've come to believe it's generally true. And even if you find exceptions, it's still useful.

Here's the principle . . .

Decisions are choices between the greater of two goods and/or the lesser of two evils from the perspective of the person facing the decision.

Notice I said, "to the person who's facing the decision." I'm not saying there aren't wrong or evil choices. There are. But we're not "moralizing" here. I'm going to resist the temptation to get philosophical and just stay focused on the issue at hand — your marriage.

Let's say you (or your wife) are mulling over: *Do I stay or go? Hang in there or give up? Stay the course or call it quits?* Come on . . . everyone thinks about it at some point!

Let's apply this "greater-of-two-goods" idea to the decision. Here's how one might look at the decision to stay or call it quits.

> **DECISIONS ARE CHOICES BETWEEN THE GREATER OF TWO GOODS AND/OR THE LESSER OF TWO EVILS FROM THE PERSPECTIVE OF THE PERSON FACING THE DECISION.**

THE "GREATER OF TWO GOODS"

Note the arguments aren't good or bad. Right or wrong. They're good versus good, at least from the perspective of the decision maker in the short-term.

Both cases are good. Which is the greater of two "goods"?

The Case for Calling It Quits

1. If I let my wife go, she'll be able to find someone who can make her happy.

2. I'll find someone else who'll understand and love me better.

3. The kids will be better off living in peace rather than this battlefield.

4. A new wife might actually make money, not just spend it.

The Case for Staying

1. I will show my kids I'm committed to marriage so they will do likewise when they grow up and get married.

2. There's a lot to be said about remaining as one family.

3. I'll feel good about myself because I stuck with it for the good of my kids.

4. It's cheaper than a divorce, alimony, child support, and another wife and family.

From the decision maker's point of view, there's good about both options. You just have to decide which offers the greater good, right?

Now let's look at it from the dark side.

THE "LESSER OF TWO EVILS"

Remember, this is from the perspective of the decision maker. He or she might think through the two evils this way:

The Case for Calling It Quits

1. My kids will grow up without both Mom and Dad in the house.

2. I'll be a "divorcee" and have to re-enter the dating scene.

3. I'll spend a fortune on the divorce, child support and funding two "households."

4. My next wife might be worse than this one.

The Case for Staying

1. We're not happy, and I don't think we ever will be.

2. Our kids are caught in the crossfire of our disagreements.

3. I have no hope my wife will ever become who I want her to be.

4. I'll live the rest of my life wondering if I could've been happier with someone else.

Can you see how our brains work? How we line up the "facts" so we don't have to wait? In the rush to get what (we think) we want *right now*, we take what looks to be the greater of two goods, connect it with the lesser of two evils and make decisions that turn out really bad in the longer term.

Robert McKee's book taught me this "greater of two goods-lesser of two evils" concept. I've changed it a little to make it useful for real life and not just storytelling:

> *"We know from life, decisions are far more difficult to make than actions are to take. We often put off doing something for as long as possible, then as we finally make the decision and step into the action, we're surprised by its relative ease. We're left to wonder why we dreaded doing it until we realize that most of life's actions are within our reach, but decisions take willpower."*[11]

Isn't it amazing how easy it is to follow your heart, to avoid hard decisions and to just "step into the action"?

LONG-TERM VERSUS WRONG TURN

So let's get real here.

In the short-term, you (or your wife) can convince yourself the greater of two goods would be to get it "over." You look at the lesser of two evils, and it seems to say the same thing. Get a divorce. Call it quits and move on.

But if you look at things long-term, it's a different story. I'm going to take each of these points and show you how different they look when you think long-term versus the wrong turn (short-term).

The "Greater of Two Goods" and the Case for Calling It Quits

Wrong Turn: *If I let my wife go, she'll find someone else who can make her happy.*

Long-term: Don't kid yourself with false altruism. She wants the man she thought you were when you married. You can become that man if you'll bury your expectations and love her — the verb love, not the noun. It'll take time.

Wrong Turn: *I'll find someone else who'll understand and love me better.*

Long-term: You may think wonderful women grow on trees, but you're in for a big surprise. The woman who'll be attracted to you will want the same things your current wife wants — *acceptance, affection, intimacy, tenderness and your time* — lots of your time. Short-term, you'll find someone who'll be infatuated with you and maybe even love you. But over the long-run, she'll want the same things your wife wants. If you can give them to a new wife, why not give them to the one you have?

And even if you do remarry, imagine your kids' weddings. There's the mother of the bride, and then there's your next wife, the stepmother (or

> **YOU LOOK AT THE LESSER OF TWO EVILS, AND IT SEEMS TO SAY THE SAME THING. GET A DIVORCE. CALL IT QUITS AND MOVE ON.**
>
> **BUT IF YOU LOOK AT THINGS LONG-TERM, IT'S A DIFFERENT STORY.**

stepmothers). There's the grandmother and the step-grandmothers. Think about the holiday celebrations — *awkward*. High school and college graduations — confusing, tense. Think about your last will and testament. College expenses. So many decisions becoming so complicated with multiple families and muddled relationships.

Wrong Turn: *The kids will be better off living in peace rather than this battlefield.*

Long-term: You and your wife can learn to deal with conflict. Again, it'll take time and effort. In the meantime, you can fight in private and commit to never letting your kids be in the middle. Sure, your kids need peace in their home. But two-parent families are the best, even if it takes years to work through the battles.

Wrong Turn: *A new wife might actually make money, not just spend it.*

Long-term: Believe it or not, money issues shrink the older you get and the longer you're married. Incomes rise; we have most of the things we need; money becomes less of an issue. And as the two of you get closer, spending decisions become more mutual.

The "Greater of Two Goods" and the Case for Staying

Wrong Turn: *I will show my kids I'm committed to marriage so they will do likewise when they grow up and get married.*

Long-term: Imagine how proud you'll feel when you and your wife celebrate your fiftieth wedding anniversary with your children and grandchildren. Think about the legacy of loyalty, devotion, commitment and forgiveness you'll pass down. It may not seem valuable right now, especially compared to the dream of being free of the problems you and your wife face. But a day will come when this stuff is "money" to you.

Wrong Turn: *There's a lot to be said about remaining as one family.*

Long-term: Imagine your family 20 years from now. All gathered around the fireplace at Christmas. You. Your wife. Your kids. Your grandkids. One meal. One house. Simple.

Wrong Turn: *I'll feel good about myself because I stuck with it for the good of my kids.*

Long-term: It will be years before your kids are old enough to appreciate how different you and your wife are and how much effort it took for you to stay together. But the message of commitment, tenacity, selflessness and forgiveness will resonate loudly from your life, speaking volumes to your kids and grandkids. (If you don't believe me, just ask a few teenagers about their parents' relationships. Pay attention to what those from broken homes have to say. Those are **your** kids' voices a few years down the road!)

Wrong Turn: *Staying's cheaper than a divorce, alimony, child support, and another wife and family.*

Long-term: You have no idea just how true this is. Men think in terms of house payments or rent, groceries and gas. I'll move out and get my own place, sounds easy enough. *Just a bed, a couch and a TV. That's all I need.* But when you move out, reality sets in. You forgot about car expenses, health insurance, school tuitions, yard maintenance and doctor bills.

You doubled your expenses because you're now supporting two families, even though one of them is just you. Add in lawyers' bills, life insurance, clothes and school activities, and you've gone so far backwards financially, it's hard to believe. You think, *Well, she'll get remarried and I'll be off the hook.* It doesn't happen that way. You'll be supporting your family to some degree from now on, regardless of what happens with your "soon-to-be" ex-wife.

Now let's think through "The Lesser of Two Evils." Does anything change here when you think long-term?

"The Lesser of Two Evils" and the Case for Calling It Quits

Wrong Turn: *My kids will grow up without both Mom and Dad in the house.*

Long-term: Teen pregnancy, alcohol abuse, drug addiction, run-ins with the law, gang membership — you name it. Every social issue is more prevalent in single-parent homes. Every one. And even if your kids escape this stuff, they're far less likely to stay married if they ever get married.

Wrong Turn: *I'll be a "divorcee" and have to re-enter the dating scene.*

Long-term: From the conversations I've had with people who are single and "single again," the dating scene is horrible and getting worse: Bitter, disillusioned, rejected and lonely women . . . rarely with balanced, healthy views of the world. Finding another wife in this culture will be harder than finding a Harvard man at a NASCAR race.

Wrong Turn: *A new wife might be worse than the one I have.*

Long-term: Your current wife won't stand still. Life will make her bitter or better. How will you feel if you skate away and she blossoms? Suppose she "finds herself," takes charge of herself and her life. Loses a few pounds. Buys some new clothes (which you will pay for) and becomes the center of some new guy's attention? There you'll be at

Johnny's Hideaway breathing the cigar smoke of other hopeless guys watching the same divorced women come to dance every weekend. Or suppose you leave your wife and find the woman you "should have married in the first place." How will things be with her after a few years? Could you end up worse than you are now?

"The Lesser of Two Evils" and the Case for Staying

Wrong Turn: *We're not happy and I don't think we ever will be.*

Long-term: You don't know the future. Your wife is capable of changing her life and becoming the woman of your dreams again. If you put her on trial, convict her and sentence her as a failure, you'll never know what she could have become. And the same applies to you. You may see yourself as a loser today. But over the long-term, you may find a job, read a book, go to a class or embrace a philosophy that will change everything for you. People never exceed parameters they set for themselves. You don't really know how you or she might change for the better.

Wrong Turn: *Our kids are "caught in the crossfire" of our disagreements.*

Long-term: Given enough time and effort, your kids could find themselves in a lovely family, led by loving parents — an *awesome, unique home.* Brought back from the "brink," everyone in the family appreciates what they have because it was almost lost.

Wrong Turn: *I'll live the rest of my life wondering if I could've been happier with someone else.*

Long-term: If you'll do what's been outlined in this book, you'll have a rare, satisfying, intimate marriage. You'll never look back and wonder what could have been because what is trumps it hands-down.

YOU GOTTA HAVE FAITH

Famous public speaker Zig Ziglar used to give a speech about this kind of faith. He had an old water pump handle he'd bring on stage, the kind people used to pump water from a well. It was the pump that made crank-handles, ropes and water buckets obsolete. It had a priming port. You had to pour water in to prime the pump to get water moving.

Zig made you close your eyes and imagine you'd been walking through the blazing-hot desert for days, so thirsty you could collapse at any moment. You come upon this pump, along with a jar of fresh water and a note. The note says:

> *"Drink this water and it will be gone. You'll save your life . . . for a while. But if you'll pour this water into the pump and prime it . . . then pump really hard for a long, long time, you'll have more water than you can imagine . . . enough to satisfy yourself and everyone with you. And you'll have plenty to refill the jar for those who'll come after you."*

Taking this most precious water — water you need and want so badly — and pouring it into what could be a "black hole" takes faith.

To pump, pump and pump some more . . . with no evidence of progress, with only hope to keep you going . . . takes commitment.

But the reward, when it comes, is refreshing and life-giving. It's everything you wanted and needed. And there's plenty for those who'll come after you.

Thinking long-term leads you to a different decision than thinking short-term. It will take commitment, selfless commitment. And the rewards? A great home. A happy marriage. Healthy, balanced kids with two parents. That's like fresh, cool water to a man dying of thirst.

And yes, being a RADICAL HUSBAND takes some faith.

STOP TALKING AND DO SOMETHING

*There comes a time in a marriage when the more
you talk about it, the more hopeless it seems.
Shut up and act.*

Leaders *initiate.* Taking responsibility for your marriage means taking the initiative. Making plans and executing. When things are great, it's easy . . . there's little risk of rejection. It's safe to lead a willing wife. When things are okay, you can quietly start doing things to grow yourself and your marriage. Fanfare isn't required, but initiative is. You can't stay asleep at the switch and just hope for a fantastic marriage. Hope is not a strategy.

But when your marriage gets in trouble, it consumes you. It can seem like you've been waist deep in "marriage stuff" forever. Long hours of tension, loneliness, worry, regret, second-guessing, and frustration, mostly with yourself. Longer hours of conversations with your wife.

Maybe you've spent eons of time with counselors. There's been so much "pathology" done on you, you feel like a medical school cadaver at the end of general anatomy. You've relived what you did, what you didn't do, what you should have done, what you could have done. You recognize her part in

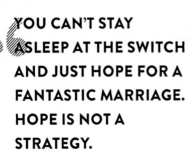

YOU CAN'T STAY ASLEEP AT THE SWITCH AND JUST HOPE FOR A FANTASTIC MARRIAGE. HOPE IS NOT A STRATEGY.

all this. Maybe she's taken half the responsibility, some responsibility or none. Even if she knows what she could have or should have done, she's not telling you. You're just tired of talking about it. You want it fixed. You want it better. You want this part of the story to end. And soon.

In his book *Love Does*, Bob Goff tells us: *"Love is never stationary. In the end, love doesn't just keep thinking about it or keep planning for it. Simply put: love does!"*[12]

So it's time to act. To move. To do *something*.

Get off by yourself and think about what you've been reading. Somewhere in a journal or on a piece of paper, write down answers to these questions.

WHAT DOES SHE LOVE?

In Step 4, I told you to "love what she loves." List what she loves down the left side of the page — everything you can think of without making up stuff. Now for each of the things she loves, brainstorm what you can do, how you can love what she loves. Scribble your ideas on the right. Here are some examples:

What She Loves	What I Can Do
Interior Decorating	Find out where home or garden tours are going on. Pick a day and ask if you can take her. Or maybe there's a cabinet she wants to paint. While she's not home, paint it for her.
Her Mother	Do what you have to do so she's free to love and serve her mother, no matter how you feel about her or how her mother feels about you.

Antiquing	She's said a few times she wants to go to this place that's "off the beaten track." Get a babysitter and take her there. *And don't rush her.* This might be bigger for her than you can imagine. So make it special by giving her plenty of browsing time.
The Kids	Take them to the zoo on Saturday morning. Make sure your wife is good with it, but completely relieve Mom of the responsibility of the kids for half a day and, at the same time, make some memories of your own. Take pictures and later make a video or slide show of the day. Make sure you are in some of the pictures, so when she sees the slideshow, she sees you *engaged* with the kids.
Your Son	Spend an evening building forts with pillows and cushions. Roughhouse with him, but make sure he doesn't get hurt. Let her see you doing "guy things" with him. A boy's dad is where he gets his first dose of masculinity. She'll sense how important that is as you give it to him.
Security	She's wanted deadbolt locks on the doors for those nights when you're out of town. Get the locks and install them, or get your carpenter friend to come over and do it. Just "get 'er done!"
Kitchen Breaks	Cook a meal for the family. Buy the groceries, cook, serve and clean up. You *can* do this!

Telling her you love her doesn't mean much. *Showing* her you love her means a lot. These illustrations are just to get you started. If you think about it long enough, you'll come up with a long list of things you can do to express your love for her. The question is, *Will you do it?*

WHAT DOES SHE NEED?

This one's a little tougher. When you think about your wife — really think about her — what does she need? Here are some possibilities:

- *More sleep.* She may be trying to function on a lot less sleep than she needs. This is a serious physical need, just as serious as good nutrition.

- *More money.* Money is the source of more disagreements than just about anything else. If she's going to do the shopping and handle the day-to-day expenses, she needs to have enough money in her budget to get the job done and not be questioned about it.

- *Help around the house.* You may have been slack about pitching in and never even known it. It's not likely, but it's possible. Laundry, dishes, kids' baths, floors and windows. Somebody has to do this stuff. She needs help.

- *Disciplinary support with the children.* Moms typically bear most of the burden of daily discipline. But they need you to back them up, to be in the game with them, especially when there's a problem brewing.

- *Her own friends.* Wives can be very lonely, especially when they don't pursue careers outside the home. They need to have adult conversations with people their own age. And they need the opportunity to do some things that are just for them.

- *Room to move around.* Just like men, women need some freedom and autonomy. When they work at home, they need to

> **TELLING HER YOU LOVE HER DOESN'T MEAN MUCH. SHOWING HER YOU LOVE HER MEANS A LOT.**

be able to get out without strollers and deadlines, just to walk around, breathe the air, shop, play tennis, hang out with friends, etc. Some may need more room than others. But every human being needs a little bit of freedom. Even prisoners in solitary confinement get a few minutes a day.

So your job is to figure out your wife's needs and meet them. Maybe not all of them. And maybe not all at once. But figuring them out and *starting to do something to meet them* will resonate deeply with her. She may start to think you actually care about her.

WHAT ARE HER DREAMS?

This might not be the time to start asking questions about her dreams. Her first answer might be to be *without you.*

But you must begin to study what she dreams about.

> **"SO YOUR JOB IS TO FIGURE OUT YOUR WIFE'S NEEDS AND MEET THEM. MAYBE NOT ALL OF THEM. AND MAYBE NOT ALL AT ONCE.**

Our marriage blew up with the statement: *We have different dreams.*

There are two possibilities here. You know her dreams, at least some of them. But you've chosen to ignore them. Discount them. Discredit them and render them as silly or unrealistic. Or you truly haven't a clue as to what she dreams about.

Here are some questions you might ask about her dreams. Please — not all at once. And maybe not even these questions. They're just here to give you a jump-start.

* *Where would you like to live now? When you're an empty nester? For retirement?*

- *What kind of house would you like to live in?*

- *What would be your dream scenario for your parents' later years? How do you see yourself (and your family) involved during those years?*

- *If you have boys: What kind of woman do you dream of them marrying?*

- *If you have girls: What kind of man do you dream of them marrying? What's your dream for our daughter's wedding?*

- *Do you dream of having a vacation home someday? Where would it be?*

- *Do you have an unfulfilled dream from your younger years? What is it? Does it still live in your heart?*

- *How would you describe your "later years" dream husband? What does he stand for? What do you love about him?*

Now this isn't Disneyland, and you can't make all her dreams come true. But you can pay attention and learn about them. You can respect them. She has a right to dream whatever she pleases. And you're an idiot if you don't make an effort to know what she dreams about. If you want a long-term, sustained, love-filled marriage relationship, you need to embrace her dreams and mesh them with your own. You may have to make some huge compromises. Your dreams and hers may be polar opposites.

> **NOW THIS ISN'T DISNEYLAND, AND YOU CAN'T MAKE ALL HER DREAMS COME TRUE. BUT YOU CAN PAY ATTENTION AND LEARN ABOUT THEM. YOU CAN RESPECT THEM.**

Dreams aren't discussed. They aren't negotiated. They're simply shared. And they'll only be confided in a husband who is "safe."

I challenge you to answer the questions posed here. If you can't, open a casual, informal dialogue with her about her dreams. Be patient. She may not want to go there right now. Wait a week. Or a month. But work your way back to it.

RADICAL HUSBANDS do stuff.

No one steers a parked car.

Move.

GIVE UP

*There's too much history, too much baggage for this to work.
You need a "new you," a "do-over," a fresh start. If you're
going to win her heart and keep it, you need help.*

Throughout the first 11 steps, there's something I haven't told you.
Something I've been holding back. I knew if I let you in on it at the
beginning, you might tune me out, stereotype me and write me off.

I also know what I've laid out here can help any married man. In fact, any man
in a committed relationship can make things better by doing what I've said.

But you can't do it. Not by yourself. Not consistently. Not for long.

How do I know?

Because I tried. I tried hard. I knew I needed to commit, to go all-in for my
wife and family. And somehow, I knew if I did, things would clear up. But I
wanted what I wanted, and I wanted it now! When I didn't "feel the love," I
compromised. I equivocated. I parsed my affection, giving some to her, but
most to my career . . . the "god" I worshipped with most of my heart and all of
my passion.

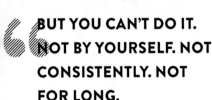

BUT YOU CAN'T DO IT. NOT BY YOURSELF. NOT CONSISTENTLY. NOT FOR LONG.

———

I'd watched other men try hard to "turn over a new leaf," go through intense counseling, lose weight, take dancing lessons, get new haircuts, buy new wardrobes — you name it. Time after time, they'd fail.

But more than a few have turned it around by doing what I did.

Are you ready for this?

I gave up.

I walked out in the backyard, looked up at a star-filled sky, and cried out to God.

On September 19, 1983, for the first time in my life, I *surrendered.*

I said:

> "God, I've made a mess of my life and my marriage. I don't like the person I am. I don't want to live like this anymore. I lie to myself, my wife, everybody. I feel like crap all the time. I want a fresh start, and I need you to help me, to change me. I'm ready to live my life a different way. I'm ready to be your man, not the man.
>
> "I'm asking you to forgive me for all I've done. And I want you to come into my life and take over. From now on, it's you and me, God; you and me. If I end up a divorced dad living in a one-bedroom apartment with my wife and kids three hours away, it's you and me, God. If she comes back and gives me another chance, it's you and me, God. Either way, I'm giving my life to you, and from here on out, it's you and me, God."

I became a Christ-follower. Not a Republican, not a church member — *an honest-to-goodness follower of Jesus Christ.*

LOVED AND DIDN'T KNOW IT

I'd heard the "gospel" all my life, the deal about God loving me. About him being pure and holy. How there was no way he could ever connect with evil. I knew there was a lot of evil in me and especially in the stuff I'd done, going all the way back to my teenage years. I knew the story about how God would forgive and give me a clean slate if I'd accept Jesus. I'd heard about the cross and how Jesus chose to sacrifice his own life to pay for my evil, allowing me to be accepted by a totally "evil-less," holy God. But somehow I knew there was more to it than that. I knew I had to be serious about it. I had to cross over a line where the gravitational pull would be toward God and away from evil. I had to embrace God and stiff-arm evil instead of continuing in evil and stiff-arming God.

That required courage and faith.

Courage had always held me back. I'd never had the backbone to say, "I'm going to do the right thing," and then do it regardless of what people thought. I was constantly looking for approval, acceptance and love. I was *compromise* walking around on two legs. I could rationalize anything.

But Miriam leaving had made me desperate. I had failed. Everyone would know. There was no way out. No way to negotiate, rationalize or equivocate. I was headed to loneliness, guilt and shame. God was my only choice, my only hope. I didn't come to him through some gallant burst of courage mustered from within. I came out of desperation. He was my only choice. Surrendering to God was my ultimate "Hail Mary" pass.

Faith came after I cried out, not before. I didn't know what would happen. I didn't know if he was really there, if he would respond or if I'd be any different.

When I went back in the house after my "God moment," I called my friend Delaine (the most committed Christian I knew) and told her what I'd asked God for. She was overwhelmed. She prayed with me and for the first time in my life, I felt like God was actually on the other end of the prayer, like he actually heard me. Over the next few days, I began to feel his presence. I felt his love. I knew the clean slate, 'do-over' thing was real.

> **FAITH CAME AFTER I CRIED OUT, NOT BEFORE. I DIDN'T KNOW WHAT WOULD HAPPEN. I DIDN'T KNOW IF HE WAS REALLY THERE, IF HE WOULD RESPOND OR IF I'D BE ANY DIFFERENT.**

But Miriam was still gone. I didn't know where. And there was no way I could make her come back. It was up to him and him alone. Only God could change her mind. After a week, she called to check on the kids. I told her of my new faith, how I'd been forgiven and started over, how I'd prayed with Delaine and how God had forgiven me. I told her how I was talking to God constantly and loving on the kids. To say she was skeptical is an understatement. But something told her (I think it was God) to at least come back and check it out.

As I mentioned earlier, she came home for one day to see if it was real. She immediately sensed something was different about me. I asked her to stay another day. She said okay. I asked for another day. Okay. Then another. That was almost 31 years ago and I'm still "day-to-day!" She's still saying "okay."

After that September night, I felt loved for the first time in my life, not by my wife, but by my heavenly Father. I didn't need Miriam's approval. I didn't need anyone's approval. I had God's. I relaxed. I knew my heavenly Father approved of me, and that was enough. I started to move toward being the man, husband and father he wanted me to be. It was "God and me." For the first time in my life, I was ready to let people know I was a Jesus-follower. Good, bad or rained out, I was "out of the closet" with my faith. I was no longer shy about my relationship with God. I was a Christian and not ashamed.

I can't overstate how life-altering it was to realize I was loved with a Father's love. He loved me because I was *his,* not because I was good. And to know his love would never go away gave me a footing I'd never had. It was a game-changer.

SPEAKING OF OUTCOMES

The other "game-changer" flowed from the first. Being sure of God's love allowed me to trust him for the outcome. Of everything. This is why I've been able to survive and even thrive in a marriage that's difficult. This may be the most significant point in this book, guys — so listen up.

With God in control, *I'm not responsible* for what happens. **God is.** I can't *make* anything happen. I'm simply responsible for doing the next right thing, and that's it. God is omnipotent. He has the power to do anything he wants. And he's omniscient — he knows everything — all the time. So an omnipotent, omniscient God . . . by definition . . . controls the outcome of everything. If I know he loves me, and I know he determines all outcomes, I can move forward doing the best I can, *trusting him for how it all turns out.* It's not up to me anymore.

Let me reconnect to my story and how this became clear to me.

When I was sitting alone in my kitchen, a seven-year-old and a ten-year-old asleep in their beds, their mom driven away by an obnoxious husband, I was powerless. Even with my new-found faith, I couldn't control the outcome. I couldn't

WITH GOD IN CONTROL, I'M NOT RESPONSIBLE FOR WHAT HAPPENS. GOD IS.

even influence it. I could pray. And pray I did. But only God could change her mind. Only God could bring her home.

A week later, he did. She'd been led to stop by the house of the friend I'd called the night I'd finally cried out to God. Delaine had given Miriam a book on marriage she'd bought just for us, not knowing that all hell had broken loose in our home. Miriam took it and read that marriage was for life, "until death do us part." God used that book to inspire her to come back and try again. God orchestrated the whole thing. I had nothing to do with her being led to come back. It was God.

ARMED WITH A THIRD PARTY

Okay, you're probably thinking, *So God loves me. And God determines outcomes. Connect the dots for me. Please. How does "giving up" help my marriage?*

First and foremost, it brings God into your situation. And he's on the side of your marriage. If it's great, he wants it to stay that way and get even better. If it's just okay, because he loves you so much and wants the very best for his children, he wants it to be wonderful. And he wants to help you save your marriage if it's in trouble. He created marriage to begin with — don't let anyone or anything tell you he wants your marriage to be over.

I started by telling you to commit to your marriage and to tell your wife you did. With God in your life, you have a "third party" involved in your marriage, a very important third party. That third party carries a lot of weight. He matters because he loves both of you. He wants it to work. Ecclesiastes 4:9–10 says,

> "*Two are better than one. . . . If either of them falls down, one can help the other up.*"[13]

Then a verse later, he says,

> "*A cord of three strands is not quickly broken.*"[14]

God is the third cord, the one who gives you the courage to make and keep your commitment. I made that commitment. Not at the altar, but at the kitchen table when I prayed on the phone with Delaine.

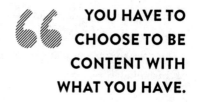

YOU HAVE TO CHOOSE TO BE CONTENT WITH WHAT YOU HAVE.

For your marriage to work, you have to make a commitment and never look back. If she opts out, you can't help that. All you can do is all you can do. Remember, God is responsible for outcomes, not you.

I told you to burn the ships, to eliminate every alternative for romance, real or imagined, other than your wife. That takes courage. Knowing you're doing what your heavenly Father wants you to do makes it easier. Knowing he'll provide companionship — through your wife and with himself — that confidence makes it possible to burn the ships.

Maybe the hardest thing I told you to do, other than giving up sex, is to drop your expectations. You have to choose to be content with what you have. "I have what I have; I get what I get. With God as my friend, I don't pitch a fit," my granddaughter says. With God as my Provider, my faith reminds me *he'll meet all my needs.* I didn't say all my wants. I said *all my needs.* Knowing that, I relax and take things as they come. I can accept Miriam as she is, knowing God accepts me just as I am.

God can set you free from your addiction to sex. Yes, addiction. Men think about sex every three minutes, and a lot of how we treat our wives comes from our desire to have sex with them. If I learn to trust God with my need for sex, it will no longer own me. When I can pray (with sincerity) . . .

> *God, I need you to help me be kind and gentle with Miriam. I need you to slow me down so I will really listen to her. I want your patience to be my patience, your gentleness to be my gentleness, my attentiveness to her to be like your attentiveness to me. Oh, and God, I'd love to have sex with her — when you decide it's time.*

When you pray that prayer and live it out, you'll be so much more intimate with your wife, and from that intimacy will come sex. The good kind. You'll become her trusted, intimate friend. Sex won't be something you push for; it'll be something that happens.

Know that you will fail over and over. It's human to want people to be and do what you want them to be and do. But it's godly to drop your expectations and accept your wife just as she is and just as she does. Do it long enough and consistently enough, and you'll create an environment of acceptance. She'll be drawn to that . . . and to you.

So much of what I've suggested rides on recognizing how much God loves you. I envy adopted children, because their parents wanted them enough to pursue them. Spending thousands of dollars and sometimes waiting for years and years, there is no questioning the love adoptive parents have for their kids.

That's the way God loves you and me. He spent the lifeblood of his only Son to pay for our sin. And now he waits for us to surrender to his love. To accept his offer of adoption into his family is to let him give us that unconditional "Father love" we so desperately seek.

Knowing you're loved like that allows you to relax and stop performing. Stop controlling. Stop manipulating. You can get into our wife's "world" and really listen to her. Not just her words, but her feelings too. You can "set her free" knowing God is in charge. That he'll take care of her. And you. You don't have anything to prove anymore, so you don't have to win every argument. Don't have to have the last word. You can "love your wife as Christ loved the church and gave *himself* up for her" (Ephesians 5:25). You can learn to lose.

Thinking long-term is different now, just like the car analogy I gave. When you commit to something, when you make it your exclusive, unconditional, never-going-to-give-you-up choice, you will start to treasure what you have and see its potential to be even greater in the future.

SO WHERE ARE YOU . . . REALLY?

See if one of these describes you:

1. You haven't surrendered and accepted God's love, although somewhere back in time, you may have said some words, prayed a prayer or gone through a confirmation class. You've depended on those words all these years, but God has made no difference in your everyday life. You've been trying to make it on your own.

2. You've always rejected Christianity out of hand. You never got it. You couldn't grasp why God would create only one way to himself. Your perception of Christians has been negative . . . and pretty accurate. The Christians you've met have been hypocritical, self-righteous and narrow-minded.

3. You're an "all-in" Jesus-follower, but you're a mess as a person. What's been laid out here as a to-do list might as well be instructions to climb Mount Everest barefooted. It's beyond your reach.

ONE STEP AT A TIME

Let me encourage you to give up. To get down on your knees and tell God you need him. Acknowledge he's God and you're not. Ask him to save you from evil and spiritual death and accept his offer of forgiveness and salvation — his offer to adopt you into his family. Forget what you prayed when you were in fifth grade. Don't depend on what your parents did, what the priest said, what your Sunday school teacher had you repeat. Connect with your heavenly Father for real. Right now. Start over. Establish *a personal relationship with God.* Start talking to him. Ask him real-time questions about what he'd have you do, how he'd have you respond and love your wife.

> **LET ME ENCOURAGE YOU TO GIVE UP.**

Think about a walk you took with someone. Maybe it was your wife or a close friend. You were right there, just a few feet from each other. There weren't a lot of words, but a closeness. A connection. Intimacy from proximity.

When you draw God close and talk openly to him, it's like that walk. You're with him and he's with you. You're praying, "Thank you for _____," "Thank you for _____," "Thank you for _____." Over and over. For everything. You're developing a heart of gratitude through personal worship, by singing a praise song to him, not about him. By singing it out loud or in your head. It doesn't matter. He hears it. He smiles. He's walking with you — *and you with him.*

And when you don't know what to do, ask and listen. Read the Bible. Ask again. Ask a committed Christian friend. Then ask again. Over time, you'll learn his ways, and you'll know what he'd have you do in almost every situation.

Then and only then will you know God is there with you and for you. Then and only then will you start making the right moves to win and keep your wife's heart. Then and only then will you have *"the peace that passes all understanding,"* a peace that *"guides your heart entirely,"* regardless of what your wife says or does.[15]

A JOURNEY OF A THOUSAND MILES

It begins with a single step. Will it be toward God? Or away from him?

If it's toward him, you have a chance to do what's been written here. Not perfectly. Not all at once. But you can move in that direction with his wind in your sails.

If it's away from him, then you're on your own. You need to read a different book, because this author's got nothing else for you. Having been on the brink looking over the edge, I will tell you that you'll be better off . . . now and forever . . . if you make the decision to turn toward him and your wife.

That's what RADICAL HUSBANDS do.

THE THIRTEENTH STEP
A MENTOR

S o I've poured it all out here. I've confessed my failures as a husband and shared what helped me recover, both personally and in my marriage. As I reflect on all that's here, one thing is missing. It was missing 44 years ago when I first got married. It was missing 31 years ago when I "ran off the rails" and my wife left. It was missing as we recovered and got things back together. And it's still missing today.

A mentor.

An older married man whose character I respect and whose marriage I admire.

So much of the pain inflicted on those I love could have been avoided if I'd had someone to talk to. Someone with real-world experience . . . who'd "been there, done that." A mentor who would have known me better than I knew myself. A courageous older friend with the balls to call me out. Ask tough questions. Make me think about the long-term consequences of decisions I was making. Back then, I never thought of having a mentor, probably because I was ashamed of who I'd become and what I was doing. My pride didn't want to have to answer to anyone or explain myself. The shame inside said, *Just keep running! Nobody will understand! Keep it to yourself. And keep moving!*

All bad advice. All lies.

I've come to see the value of having a mentor, and while I can't make up for the missing mentor in my life, I can be that mentor to young married guys I know. I've discovered that older men love helping younger ones. It's part of their wiring. Part of their innate calling to want to give back. Younger men who reach out to older guys are *rarely turned down*. But they do have to ask, and that takes a big serving of humility. When you reach out to a potential mentor, you're admitting (in a way) that you don't know it all. That you might need some help. It's a little like asking for directions. It's hard to bring yourself to.

But the rewards can be infinite, both for you and for the guy who mentors you. You get challenged, perspective, helpful suggestions, experience and insight. He gets meaning, fulfillment and purpose in his life. It's a win-win.

So how do I find this "legendary" mentor-person?

Think through the married men you know. Your criteria are pretty simple . . . who do you respect and look up to? Who has a long-term marriage that looks like the one you want? Who seems to be the kind of husband you'd like to be? Who reflects the character you want to have when you're his age?

Pick up the phone and call him. Tell him you read this book about being a great husband, and the author suggested reaching out to a man whose marriage and character you admire. Ask if he'll meet you for coffee or lunch. Don't "spring" anything on him. Don't ask him to be your marriage mentor. Just spend a little time with him and see "up close and personal" if he's the kind of guy you'd like to be mentored by. See if he's a talker or a listener. Talkers make bad mentors. Listeners . . . just the opposite.

You may have to buy two or three lunches before you make the friend who's going to walk with you in your marriage. You don't necessarily need a program or a curriculum or an agenda. You need a respected friend who'll spend a little time with you from time to time.

Eventually, you may want to formalize your mentoring relationship. You might suggest pulling together a few other guys (your age and station in life) and do a more formal mentoring season together. Your mentor might get a little nervous about taking on more than one of you, but if you're benefitting from his help, he might be willing to take the risk of mentoring a small group of similar guys for a period of time.

That's what I do as a mentor. I "walk with" a group of younger married guys every year, personally sharing with them what I've shared with you in this book. The learning that takes place . . . the camaraderie that develops . . . the way we grow as husbands and fathers . . . it blows my hair back. The "how to" of these *Radical Mentoring Groups* is available free at WWW.RADICALMENTORING.COM.

And one more option.

We've created a website just for men who want to become radical husbands. You'll find marriage exercises there, perfect to do on your own or to work through with a group of guys. We've laid these out to be done one at a time . . . to work on one single aspect of your marriage for a month, then come back together to talk about what happened and what you learned. Check it out at WWW.RADICALHUSBANDS.COM.

AFTERWORD

"I hope what you've read here will be helpful to you. It's been a mission of love for Regi. He's worked really hard on this because he genuinely wants you to work things out in your marriage. What you've read here is what I've heard him share over and over with the men he mentors around our dining room table. He's passionate — to say the least.

"Regi and I have been married for almost 45 years. Looking back, those early years are pale memories. When I was young, I never believed a person could change — really change. For a time, I felt trapped in a marriage with someone who was extremely insensitive and selfish. The pain was daily. I never believed I would look back and see good come from those years, but I was wrong.

"When I left and then came back, the change in Regi was noticeable. I felt his love for me in a different way. Many, many times my responses to him were hurtful, but he continued to show me love. I watched as he became 'present' in our family. I watched as he took more time with our kids. I noticed when he came home in time for family dinners. That was extremely important to me.

"Pain is something you feel intensely in the present. As time goes on, you remember it, but it doesn't hurt like it did in the beginning. Looking back, I am so thankful that we worked on making our marriage last. At the time, I'm not sure we recognized how much we had to lose.

"I look at my grown son and daughter now, and think how different their lives would have been if we hadn't hung in and made it work. I look in the faces of my beautiful and innocent grandchildren and know their lives have not been damaged by my unwillingness to forgive. And then I look in the face of my dear, sweet husband and think about the blessings I would have missed if we had not committed to finish our lives together.

"It hasn't been smooth sailing. It was incredibly hard because we were, and still are, so different. But I recognize that as unique creations, we react to circumstances in ways that are familiar to us. He's 'just Regi' and I'm 'just Miriam.' We're learning to accept each other and even value our differences. But to say it's been easy or without pain wouldn't be true.

"The stumbling blocks in your life and marriage now will not be so important when you look back years from now. Things will change. Things that matter so much now won't matter at all later on. And things that are so easy to ignore and overlook right now will be very important down the road.

"We have learned a lot about ourselves over these years. I can now see how we got to where we were. But at the time, we were clueless. I encourage you to give your husband, yourself and your marriage the gift of time — it's such a great teacher!

"We look back now with no regrets. There were many things we could have done better, but we know we tried. We've set the best example we could for our kids and grandkids. They know we had a rough time, but they also know we hung in there and worked it out.

"I hope you decide to hang in there. If Regi and I, being so different, can stay married and enjoy it, I know you can too."

— MIRIAM CAMPBELL

Regi's wife

FOOTNOTES

1. "Ruth Bell Graham: A Life Well Lived, Part 2," *Decision,* June 2013

2. Karyn Loscocco1,* and Susan Walzer - Gender and the Culture of Heterosexual Marriage in the United States -†Journal of Family Theory & Review, Volume 5, Issue 1, pages 1–14, March 2013

3. Andy Stanley, *Next Generation Leader* (Colorado Springs, CO: Multnomah Books, 2003), 51

4. Glen Clark, *The Man Who Talked with the Flowers: The Life Story of Dr. George Washington Carver* (Minnesota: Macalester Park Publishing Company, 1934, 1994)

5. Bill Graham, Robert Greenfield, *Bill Graham Presents – My Life Inside Rock and Out* (Cambridge, MA., Da Capo Press, 1992) 423

6. John Eldredge, You Have What it Takes (Nashville, TN: Thomas Nelson, 2004), 3

7. Jason S. Carroll, Laura M. Padilla-Walker, Larry J. Nelson, Chad D. Olson, Carolyn McNamara Barry, Stephanie D. Madsen; "Generation XXX: *Pornography Acceptance and Use Among Emerging Adults," Journal of Adolescent Research* (Vol. 23 No. 1, January 2008), 6-30

8. Rand Scott Marquardt, The Fairway of Life: Simple Secrets to Playing Better Golf by Going with the Flow (Bloomington, IN: iUniverse, 2009), 408

9. *Proceedings of the National Academy of Sciences,* DOI: 10.1073pnas.0803081105

10. Gordon McDonald, *Rebuilding Your Broken World* (Nashville TN: Thomas Nelson, 1988, 1990, 2003)

11. Robert McKee, *Story: Style, Structure, Substance and the Principles of Screenwriting* (Harper Collins, Inc. Kindle Edition: 2010), 304

12. Bob Goff. *Love Does* (Nashville, TN: Thomas Nelson, 2012)

13. Ecclesiastes 4:9, Holy Bible, New International Version, International Bible Society, 1973, 1978, 1984

14. Ecclesiastes 4:10, Holy Bible, New International Version, International Bible Society, 1973, 1978, 1984

15. Philippians 4:7, Holy Bible, New International Version, International Bible Society, 1973, 1978, 1984

BE A
RADICAL
HUSBAND

Access additional marriage exercises

Share your own experiences

Hear what others are doing

Give feedback to the author

Arrange for Regi to speak to
your group

Help spread the word and build a
movement of Radical Husbands!

RADICALHUSBANDS.COM

9 780991 607402